All In This Together

Also by Jack Kornfield

No Time Like the Present

Meditation for Beginners

A Path with Heart

The Wise Heart

The Art of Forgiveness, Lovingkindness, and Peace

A Lamp in the Darkness: Illuminating the Path Through Difficult Times

After the Ecstasy, the Laundry

Bringing Home the Dharma

Teachings of the Buddha

The Buddha Is Still Teaching: Contemporary Buddhist Wisdom

A Still Forest Pool

Seeking the Heart of Wisdom

Soul Food

Living Dharma

Buddha's Little Instruction Book

All In This Together

Stories and Teachings for Loving Each Other and Our World

Jack Kornfield

BOULDER, COLORADO

Sounds True
Boulder, CO

© 2025 Jack Kornfield

Sounds True is a trademark of Sounds True Inc.
All rights reserved. No part of this book may be used or reproduced in any manner without written permission from the author(s) and publisher.

No AI Training: Without in any way limiting the author's and publisher's exclusive rights under copyright, any use of this publication to "train" generative artificial intelligence (AI) technologies to generate text is expressly prohibited. The author reserves all rights to license uses of this work for generative AI training and development of machine learning language models.

Every effort has been made to identify the source of each story and obtain permission when necessary. Please see the Notes and Permissions for details.

Published 2025

Cover and jacket design by Rachael Murray
Book design by Charli Barnes

Permissions credit lines listed in back

Printed in Canada

BK07158

Cataloging-in-Publication data for this book is available from the Library of Congress.

ISBN: 9781649633569

eBook ISBN: 9781649633576

*To my beloved wife and life partner, Trudy.
Your wisdom and depth, playful spirit, and
shining heart brought me into a field of love
that has changed the story of my life.*

*And to Desmond, who at 6 loves a good story.
May all your stories be good.*

Sometimes a person needs
a story more than food.

BARRY LOPEZ

Contents

Introduction	1
The Respectful Heart: We Are All in This Together	3
Generosity of Vision: Nothing Will Change, Unless We Can Envision It	39
Healing and Freedom: The Power of the Listening Heart	93
To Serve and to Care: Skillful Service and a Loving Heart	143
Mystery, Death, and Consciousness: Oh Nobly Born, Remember Who You Really Are	207
Notes	259
Permissions	265
About the Author	269

The universe is made of stories,
not of atoms.

MURIEL RUKEYSER

Introduction

WE ALL WANT a good story. Especially in trying times, our cultures need stories to inspire us, educate us, touch us, and bring us together. Shared stories make us larger than ourselves. The revered books of ancient times—the Bible, the Greek plays, the Japanese *Tale of Genji*, the Mayan Popol Vuh, the Koran, the Bhagavad Gita—are filled with stories.

Remember when you were a kid and how great it was to hear a good tale, whether it was read to you at bedtime or you saw it on television or heard it at school? Now I have the delight of offering some more tales to you. I am a lover of stories, and I have been collecting them all my life. I tell them, write them, teach from them, and pass them on.

Look for the magic in the tales included here. Look for their message. In the first story, there is guidance on respect from King Arthur's time. In the last story we encounter teachings from the Buddha on coming together to build a wise society. Throughout, you will find inspiration for conflict resolution and powerful stories of healing and justice and human kindness and compassion.

These tales invite us into an illuminating, intimate, and universal realm that can touch the heart and awaken revelation and understanding. Some of the stories here are ancient; some are new. Some come from my travels and some from our global shared wisdom. All these stories are quintessentially human and equally timeless, and we need them now more than ever.

Relax as you read. And enjoy.

Go slowly. Savor.

Let the stories be reminders of who you really are.

Notice how they touch the compassion and freedom that is already in your heart.

Let them move you and wake you up and remind you: We are all in this together.

With blessings,

JACK KORNFIELD

Spirit Rock Meditation Center

The Respectful Heart

We Are All
in This Together

How far you go in life depends on your being tender with the young, compassionate with the aged, sympathetic with the striving, and tolerant of the weak and the strong. Because someday you will have been all of these.

GEORGE WASHINGTON CARVER

TAKE A MOMENT to remember what it is like to be treated with respect. Remember how it is to be listened to with care—and how important it is to offer this same kindness to yourself and others.

Let us start with a wise olde story that calls us to understand.

One summer afternoon, Sir Gawain, one of the youngest and most gallant knights of King Arthur's round table, was traveling through Arthur's kingdom in the countryside when he entered a dark and tangled forest. Alas, he got lost among the enormous trees and vines and creepers of this dark wilderness, and the cold night fell before he could find his way out.

Alive with the hollers and hoots of the night creatures, the shadowy forest closed in on Sir Gawain and he found himself stuck among the roots and thorns and brambles. Even his great horse was unable to free him. Only when the light of the stars and moon lit up the wood was Gawain able to tear himself free. Still lost, he walked on and eventually came upon a clearing. A bit of moonlight shone through the clouds, and a beautiful well appeared in the middle of a clearing. *At least I can rest here and satisfy my thirst*, he thought.

When he drew the bucket up from the well and drank from it, his thirst was quenched and he made himself a place to rest by his horse. In the night distance, he heard the slightest pitter-patter. *An oncoming rain*, he thought. But as the sound grew louder, he bolted up from his rest, recognizing it as the sound of hooves from an approaching horse. *Who else had wandered this deep through such a dark and tangled wood?* he wondered.

Suddenly, a great white stallion was upon him and on it was a woman with beautiful long hair and a deep red cloak. Slowly, she turned and pulled the cloak's hood from her head. Above him on the horse sat a hag. Her teeth were yellowed, rotting, or missing, and her skin was crevassed, boiled, and scarred. A bit of a beard hung off her pointy chin, and one of her eyes looked directly at him as the other strayed. Her hair was matted and had the consistency of straw.

The hag slid off her horse and crouched down in her velvet cloak to meet him. Gawain, a man of great courtesy, bowed.

"It is a pleasure to make your acquaintance, madam," he said.

"You drank from my well," she said.

Gawain immediately replied with regret, "I'm sorry, madam."

"Is that all a great knight has to say?" she asked. "Can't you do better than that?"

Sir Gawain lowered his head, noting her mysterious power. "If I've offended you in any way, I will do whatever I can as a knight to make up for it."

"I thank you for that promise," she replied, "and there is something that you can do to make up for it."

"Whatever you wish."

The hag paused a moment, then continued, "I'm finding myself to be rather lonely, and so I would like to have a husband. You would make a perfect mate. Let us wed."

Gawain gulped, but as a knight he knew the gravity of a promise. He knew he must keep it.

"Yes, I would like a big wedding," the hag said. "I envision it at Arthur's castle where we invite everyone in the kingdom to come."

"Couldn't we have a little private one?" Gawain asked.

"Oh no, no, no. We have to do this right," she said, noting

Gawain's reservation, which was now bordering on desperation.

"Isn't there anything else I could do for you?" he pleaded.

"Well, I suppose there is one other small thing," the hag said, the slightest twinkle in her bulging and wayward eye. "If you can find the true answer to one question and return here with the correct answer, let's say in one year, then I will absolve you of your offense and free you from your promise to marry me."

"Certainly, your ladyship. What is the question?"

With one eye, the old woman looked directly at him.

"What is it that women want?" she asked.

Gawain took a breath. A hard question. He did not know the answer or even how to find it, but he knew about quests. And he would keep his promise. "Of course, madam," he said. "I will find the answer to your question."

The old hag did not linger. She got back on her horse and disappeared into the dark of the forest, leaving Gawain to wait out the night alone. When he awoke in the morning, it was as if the forest had been parted open. He found his way easily out of the tangled woods and into the light.

When he returned, he gathered King Arthur and the other knights and told them what had happened. "I must answer this question," he told them.

He procured a great book, old and leather bound, which he would use as a sort of ledger. Then he went with his minions around the country interviewing women, asking each of them what they wanted. Some wanted wealth, some wanted many children, some wanted love, some wanted a nice piece of land, some wanted a horse, and some wanted a fine meal. Gawain wrote every single answer down and by the end of the year, he'd filled the large leather volume. He packed it on his steed and rode back to the middle of the tangled forest. Once again he sat by the well as the moon rose. And sure enough, he soon heard the sound of horse's hooves coming toward him, and the cloaked hag soon arrived.

"Well, have you got an answer?" she asked.

Sir Gawain took a knee as he handed her the book. "I have a thousand answers," he said.

The hag flipped through it, and as she did so, she shook her head and said, "No, no, no, no, no, no. I'm sorry but you do not have the answer here."

Gawain's heart fell, and he was filled with dread as he looked up at the hag.

"When shall we have the wedding?" she asked. "Let's do it right away!"

"Well, can we postpone it for a little while?" Gawain responded weakly.

"Fine," she said, "How about next week?"

"How about in two weeks?" he said. But what did it matter? They would be married. He had agreed.

This time, the two returned to the castle together, and in spite of Sir Gawain's reluctance, the wedding took place, complete with the feast, old wine, and music. All the grand things that happened in Arthur's court happened in this great wedding between the hag and Sir Gawain. And when it was done, they retired to the bridal chamber.

Seated on the side of the bed, Sir Gawain's new bride patted the soft blanket next to her, inviting him to come and sit close to her. "Aren't you going to kiss the bride?" she asked.

Sir Gawain hesitated, eying the yellow substance oozing out

of the boils on her cheek.

The hag held his gaze. "You are a brave knight after all, are you not?"

Sir Gawain took a deep breath, then leaned over and touched his lips to hers. As their lips met, the hag turned into a gloriously beautiful young woman who had always been a princess. A reward for Gawain's knightly gesture. Gawain held her face in his palms and gazed at his stunning and radiant bride.

"Ah, I'm so glad we're married now," he said.

"But there is one problem that remains," she said. "Your kiss has released me from a terrible spell that I have been under and now I am free but only half so. I can be in my beautiful form for only half the time. My beauty will remain at night with you in our bed chamber, but in the daytime, I will resume the form of a hag. Or, if you wish, I can be beautiful by your side during the day and at nighttime I will turn into the hag. Which do you choose, dear husband?"

Facing a great dilemma like life offers us on occasion, Gawain spent some time reflecting. He got quiet. He listened deeply. As he looked at her, this beautiful new bride in front of him, he felt the love that reflected his care that was only growing.

"I cannot choose for you," he said. "I place this decision in your hands. What would you choose?"

In this moment, her eyes lit up. She grew brighter, and even more beautiful.

"Now you have broken the whole spell," she said. "The answer to the question that I asked you at the very beginning has now been revealed from your own lips. What do women want? They want what every human wants: their sovereignty. They wish to be free from having someone else say, 'You must do this and you must be that, and you should do this and you shouldn't do that.' We all want to be honored in our own right for who we are. What women—and all humans—want most is respect. And you have given me this."

As you might imagine, Sir Gawain and Dame Ragnelle (for this was her name) went on to have a sweet wedding night followed by a long happy marriage filled with love, respect, and mutual care.

❖

Loving respect for oneself, for others, and for the world around us is the foundation of a wise society. Everyone wants respect. Your partners want it, your friends want it, as do your children and parents, your colleagues and your pets, and your gardens and your neighbors. All thrive on loving respect. It is central to the practice of awakening and the liberation of the heart.

When we approach the world wisely, we must begin with respect. And while we may lose our way, we can always return to respect. You can always pause and ask yourself, *Am I present with respect?*

We are born with basic goodness and a heart of compassion, a capacity to live in a respectful way. When we treat ourselves and those we meet with caring attention and respect, this simple act brings freedom and dignity to ourselves and others. It bestows a blessing of sovereignty to you and all that you touch.

A SEVEN-YEAR-OLD BOY went out with his mother and father to a restaurant. The waitress came and took their orders. First she asked the boy, who looked up at her eagerly, "What will you have?"

"I'd like a hot dog and a coke," the boy answered.

His mother immediately corrected him. Turning to the waitress, she said, "He'll have the meatloaf, the mashed potatoes, and a glass of milk."

The waitress continued to go around the table, getting everyone's orders and writing them down. Ready to leave, she paused for a moment. Then she turned to the boy and said, "Would you like ketchup or mustard on your hot dog?"

As she walked away, the little boy turned to his parents and said, "She thinks I'm real."[1]

❁

I love the Buddhist texts that begin with phrases like this: "Oh noble one, do not forget who you really are." In other words, do not forget your dignity. Do not forget the dignity of others. Remember the heart of compassion and wisdom that was born into you.

PEOPLE TRAVELED great distances to ask the Buddha for teachings, which he always offered willingly. Sometimes he would give very demanding teachings and other times softer, loving teachings that enfolded you in their care. It depended on the needs of the questioner.

Whenever the Buddha was done with his teaching, he would look at the questioners as they digested their lessons, and then he would conclude with a famous phrase: "Now it is time for you to do as you see fit." It was as if he was saying, "My friends, I've given you the best teachings that I can. I've illuminated what can be seen, and now I place these in your heart, in your hands." This was a gesture of respect and sovereignty.

When you read or hear wise teachings from the Buddha or other sages, what should you do next? Reflect. Consider. Listen to your own heart for "it is time for you to do as you see fit." You are the one who determines how you will live.

IN THE FOREST MONASTERY where I lived with my teacher, Ajahn Chah, the entire community was built around the respectful heart. The paths in the forest were swept with care and attention to beauty. We were taught how to mindfully fold our robes, to carefully clean our alms bowls, and to bow to one another. With every gesture, we offered our respect and received respect from others. This field of loving care allowed us to be present for each other and all the creatures of the forest—the small deer, the wild hens, the civets, and the cobra—all in beautiful ways.

The natural world—quails and ants, oaks and owls—loves and needs our respect. Lloyd Reynolds, the celebrated American calligrapher (and inspiration to Steve Jobs), reminds us of this in his artful lettering:

> *A bug crawls over the paper,*
> *leave him be,*
> *we need all the readers we can get.*

The bugs want your respect, too.

PRACTICING AS MONKS, we were trained to bow three times upon entering and leaving the temple. Bowing was a new experience for me. We were instructed to bow when we entered and exited the dining hall, the teachers' quarters, even our own huts.

One day I was taught it is proper for a monk to kneel and bow three times when he encounters a monk who is senior to him. Being newly ordained, this meant bowing to every monk I met. At first this was difficult. There were monks I respected who were easy to bow to, but at other times I found myself bowing to monks I thought clueless, proud, or unworthy. To bow to some of these fellows simply because they had been ordained a month or two before me rubbed me the wrong way. In my mind, they had not yet earned my respect. However, I continued to bow in the temple, in my hut, and to all the monks who presented themselves to me.

After some time, I felt the painful spirit of my own criticism. So I began to pause and secretly look for something that was worthy in each person I met. I honored the wrinkles around the eyes of a grumpy old monk and imagined all he had lived through. I saw the creative potential in a prideful young monk who at first seemed just full of himself. I gradually noticed that every single being carries some aspect worthy of respect. Then I began to enjoy bowing to them. I would bow to every monk, to the temples, to all my brothers and sisters, to the trees, and to the rocks. Bowing became a joyful way of being.[2]

ONCE I WAS RIDING in a small pickup with Ajahn Chah to visit a distant forest monastery on the Cambodian border. A young layman had offered us a ride. He liked to speed, as young men do.

The problem was that the long drive was on a one-and-a-half-lane dirt road winding through the southern mountains. The road was mostly empty, but occasionally as we turned a curve there'd be a bus or a logging truck or a water buffalo taking up the entire road. Yet our driver just kept speeding around the blind corners.

We asked him to slow down, but he did not do so. I held on tight and thought, *Okay, I might die as a monk here on this ride.* And it just got worse. There was a drop-off on one side, and you couldn't see what was coming. I looked over and I saw that my teacher's knuckles were white too. Somehow this reassured me. I don't know why.

Finally we made it to the monastery. As we pulled into the courtyard of the forest clearing and temple, Ajahn Chah turned to me, smiled, and said, "Scary ride, wasn't it?"

While for me the ride had triggered all kinds of reactions, for him, it was simply a "scary ride." It was then that I realized it isn't that a great master isn't supposed to be scared; it's that he just offered a bow to the simple truth and acknowledged it for what it is.

IN MY STUDY I HAVE a treasured photograph of a meeting between His Holiness the Dalai Lama and Maha Ghosananda, the Gandhi of Cambodia—both celebrated as exemplars of compassion.

The photo captures a beautiful moment. Old friends, they had just come together at the Spirit Rock Meditation Center, where the Dalai Lama was visiting. As they bowed to one another, they each tried to bow lower than the other. They bowed lower, and lower, and lower until finally their heads bumped as they grew closer to the earth. All to offer each other their respect.

May we all be so gracious to one another that we end up closer to the earth.

We are sun and moon, dear friend;
we are sea and land. It is not our purpose
to become each other; it is to recognize
each other, to learn to see the other
and honor him for what he is: each the
other's opposite and complement.

HERMANN HESSE

THE TIBETAN LAMA Sakyong Mipham was staying with friends in Colorado. A great horseman, he decided to spend the day wandering the Rocky Mountain wilderness on horseback. As he tells it, "I took one of my favorite horses, Rocky, on a trail ride through some backcountry. I had ridden Rocky before, mostly in the arena. He was a very intelligent horse, but he didn't know how to walk a trail. It was a new situation—for him and for me. I was leading the group, and that also made him a little nervous. I coaxed him over certain big rocks and shifted my weight to indicate to him how to go around certain others, but he kept stumbling.

"We came to a narrow place in the trail. On one side was a steep shale cliff and on the other, a long drop into the river. Rocky stopped and waited for my direction. We both knew that one wrong move would plummet us into the river far below. Gently I guided him toward the gorge, while subtly shifting my weight toward the high wall of shale. I thought that if he slipped, I could jump off and save myself.

"The moment I shifted to prepare for such a scenario, Rocky stopped cold and craned his head around to look at me. He knew *exactly* what I was doing. I could tell he was shocked and hurt that I was planning to abandon him. The look in his eye said, 'You and me together, right?' Seeing how terrified he was, I shifted my weight back. He swung his head forward in relief and we negotiated the trail together with no problems."[3]

DURING ONE OF CALIFORNIA'S big climate summits in San Francisco, we held a climate day at Spirit Rock. There I had a dialogue with Christiana Figueres, a remarkable woman and a diplomat from Costa Rica, who for years had been the United Nations special representative for climate change.

Christiana said that as she'd been working to organize the Paris Climate Summit, she had grown more and more depressed, undermined, and discouraged in her activism. There had been growing pushback on the science of climate change, and some of the players involved in the politics behind climate change were resisting and undermining all the good work. Some of these folks—the nations and corporations and their leaders—played the role of "bad actors" and personified greed and tragedy as if in a Shakespearean play. But it wasn't just the leaders that made her feel such despair. In her mind, every one of us had played a part, and many of us had become indifferent or recalcitrant as well.

Christiana didn't know what to do. The Paris Climate Accords were approaching, and her heart was heavy. Just a few months before the meeting, someone said to her, "Go and see Thich Nhat Hanh, the Vietnamese Zen Master, at Plum Village in France. He will help you." She had never heard of him, but desperate, she went.

There they taught her meditation and the teachings of interdependence. They offered practices on the great heart of compassion, which illuminated how we are all a part of everything. And if you have ever been with Thich Nhat Hanh and seen him walk, you know how it changes your life. Your whole body goes, "Wow! That's what it means to walk mindfully." His walk is intense and wonderful. He's amazingly present. After walking with the students, he sits down with a calm and very deep sense of presence and conversation. He embodies what it means to be present on the earth.

Christiana walked and sat with him, and all of this began to soothe her heart. She began to understand, as she listened to the teachings, how interconnected we are, that every breath and every drink of water are shared. The earth that we walk on is shared. We are all in this together. Thich Nhat Hanh, and his practices and presence, revived her spirit. He helped her to realize that there's another way of seeing the divides we find ourselves in.

"When I went back to lead the Paris Climate Accords, I was in a completely different place," Christiana said. "Everyone was in their own corner. Everyone was blaming and struggling against the other. The paradigm was that there are victims and the perpetrators. Which countries were doing it to whom? But through the wisdom from my practice, I was able to shift the narrative so that instead of talking about victims and perpetrators, I talked about interdependence. I talked about how we are all part of one big family. This shift in my own consciousness and in the narrative allowed me to help all 196 countries to sign on to the Paris Climate Accords."

IN THE EARLY YEARS of the Iraq war, there was a story in *The New Yorker* about a small unit of American soldiers who were assigned to go to the holy city of Najaf. This was a delicate mission, as the presence of the Americans in uniform was seen as a desecration of their sacred sites. When they approached one of the most revered mosques, hundreds of Iraqis poured out of the buildings on either side, fists waving, throats taut. They pressed in on the fifteen Americans, who glanced at one another in terror. The reporter witnessing it said he felt afraid that a shot would come from somewhere. Someone would open fire, and it would turn into a massacre.

Then, quite suddenly in the middle of it all, the American officer in charge stopped and held his rifle high over his head with the barrel pointed to the ground. He stood there against the backdrop of the seething crowd, now almost a thousand deep. It was a striking gesture, almost biblical. And then he took a knee. The officer, his eyes hidden behind mirrored sunglasses, held his position and told his men to follow. The other soldiers looked at him as if he were crazy, and then, one after the other, swaying in their bulky body armor and gear, they knelt before the boiling crowd, pointed their guns at the ground in the same position as their officer. The Iraqis fell silent—and their anger subsided. The officer ordered his men to withdraw.

Dan Baum, the writer of the story, said it took him months to track down Lieutenant Colonel Chris Hughes, the officer in the account. When he found him, he asked Hughes who had taught him to calm a crowd by pointing his rifle down and kneeling in a war zone in a distant country.

Hughes replied that while they would typically fire warning shots in such a situation, the problem with doing so is that the next thing that happens is that people start shooting for real. He went on to say that the Iraqis felt that the presence of these armed Americans was disrespectful to their mosque and the culture in the holy city—and that the obvious solution was a gesture of respect.[4]

He who wants a rose
must respect her thorn.

PERSIAN PROVERB

WHEN AJAHN CHAH was a young monk, he lived out in the jungles among wild animals—elephants, boar, and even tigers. He stayed in the caves, meditated through bouts of malaria and dysentery, suffered physical pain, and went through the outer struggles that one has as a strict renunciate. All to find an unshakable peace within himself.

And he found it.

His instructions as a teacher were born from his time in the jungle. He talked very simply about "taking the one seat." "Just go into your forest hut and take the one seat in the center of the room," he said. "Open the doors and windows and see who comes to visit. In meditation you'll witness all kinds of scenes and actors, pleasures and pains, temptations and stories, everything imaginable. Your only job is to stay in your seat. To respect everything that comes with kindness and equanimity. You'll see it all arise and pass. And out of your steady presence, wisdom, compassion, and true freedom will arise."

A FRIEND OF MINE, Arturo Bejar, was the director of engineering at Facebook for six years. Part of his job included tending to the problems that came up on the social media channel. He was basically the complaints department.

During his time, Facebook already had a billion users. "At this size it didn't take very long to get a million complaints," he said.

"What did you do?" I asked him.

"Well, a third of the problems were technical complaints. I gave those problems to the engineers; they fixed them. That's what engineers do, no problem. But most of the complaints had to do with conflicts and blame between users of Facebook like 'You posted a picture of me and I don't look good.' And 'How dare you post a picture of my children without permission?' And 'You said this about me, and you only heard it secondhand from other people.'

"As a first step, I sent the complainers the corporate rules. Our company policy was that if someone has posted something lewd or lascivious or hateful, then we take it down. Otherwise, we leave it. But unfortunately this didn't solve anything. No one was happy.

"I thought, *There's got to be a better way.* So I began to experiment. I recommended to those who complained that instead of responding with blame and judgment they try to be more curious and interested. To those who were complaining about someone else, I sent out a message that said, 'Why don't you ask them what made them do it? What was their motivation? And why don't you tell them how it made you feel? Frustrated? Angry? Betrayed? Sad?'

"Then I found out that many people don't know what they feel, so I sent out little emoticons: faces for happy, sad, angry, confused, and irritated. I wrote, 'Use these to tell them how it made you feel. And then ask them the question, What made you do what you did?'"

The result was astonishing. My friend Arturo explained to me that now the people responded differently. Instead of complaining, they engaged. He received reports like "When I asked why the person posted that horrible picture of me, the poster responded and said, 'Sorry, I thought you looked good in that picture.'" And "I posted your children because I love your children. And I thought other people would want to see this beautiful picture."

Arturo said that 90 percent of the conflict was eliminated when people began to talk to each other respectfully. Smiling, he said, "I got to teach social and emotional learning and conflict resolution to 980 million people."

When we listen kindly to those around us, we open a channel to their own goodness. We can see the best in one another. Listening with curiosity and care transforms everyone's hearts.

AS HE MOVES THROUGH THE WORLD, the Dalai Lama holds the sacred perception of respect. It is one of the reasons so many people seek to be around him.

Several years ago, after His Holiness visited San Francisco, we invited him to offer teachings at Spirit Rock. The Dalai Lama is the head of the Tibetan government in exile, so the State Department had assigned dozens of Secret Service agents to protect him and his entourage. Accustomed to guarding foreign leaders, princes, and kings, the Secret Service agents were surprisingly moved by the Dalai Lama's respectful attitude and friendly heart. At the end, they asked for his blessing. Then they all wanted to have a photo taken with him. Several said, "We have had the privilege of protecting political leaders, princes, and prime ministers, yet there is something different about the Dalai Lama. He treats us as if we are special."

Later, during a series of public teachings, he stayed at a classic San Francisco hotel famous for hosting dignitaries. Just before he departed, the Dalai Lama told the hotel management that he would like to thank the staff in person. So on the last morning, a long line of maids and dishwashers, cooks and maintenance men, secretaries and managers made their way to the great circular driveway at the hotel entrance. And before the Dalai Lama's motorcade left, he walked down the line of employees, lovingly touching each hand, vibrating the strings of each heart.

If we lose love and respect for each other,
this is how we will finally die.

MAYA ANGELOU

ONCE, I WORKED WITH extraordinary mythologist Michael Meade and renowned poet Luis Rodriguez offering retreats for young men who were trying to get out of street gangs in Oakland, Chicago, and Los Angeles. The guys came in with their hoods up and their heads down. You could hear what they were thinking: *You're going to do some poetry and teach me some meditation and shit like that. Come on man, I'm on the street. People got guns. You got to give me something better than that.*

We lit a candle and put it in the center of a table and said, "There are too many people with us who haven't been acknowledged and who need our respect. Please go out to the parking lot and collect a stone for every young person you know who's been killed. Then put the stones by this candle and say their names."

Each of the youths left and returned. Some of their hands were full of stones. "This is for RJ and this is for Tito and this one for Homegirl Leena." So many names were said. And when the stones were piled up next to the candle, we sat quietly. The room had changed. Hoods came down, hats came off. They were ready to talk about their lives. They were ready to get real.

TO LIVE WITH TENDERNESS and an open heart, along with its magnificence and beauty, we also have to respect the difficult truths of the world—the reality of pain and loss and suffering. We have to respect the fact that people are frightened and hungry, that those we love will die, and that there are fourteen thousand nuclear warheads on this earth, before we can do anything about any of it. We can't pretend these facts are not true. We must let the reality of these truths in and offer a respectful bow and only then say, "What can we do? What are the steps we must take to respond?"

Respect for the truth—a bow rather than denial—guides us to step forward wherever we are called: to help the elderly, the young, the teens, the disenfranchised, the rich or the poor, or the Palestinians, Israelis, Hutus, Tutsies, Christians, Muslims, Buddhists, Jews, and atheists. We can start simply, listening with our hearts and respecting the truth of the situation. Honoring the suffering around us and offering the world our kind attention opens us to find a wise and caring response.

SOME YEARS AGO, the great primate biologist George Schaller came back from studying gorillas in Africa. Schaller was the mentor of the primatologist and conservationist Dian Fossey, who was portrayed by Sigourney Weaver in the movie *Gorillas in the Mist*. When Schaller returned from his field studies, he made a presentation at an important biological conference and talked about the familial patterns of the great apes. He spoke about the relationships between the young gorillas and their uncles and aunts and siblings and the role of the silverback male—all with rich detail and understanding that had never been known before.

One of the professors at the conference asked, "Dr. Schaller, biologists have been studying these creatures for several centuries, and we did not know any of this. How did you get such detailed information?" And Professor Schaller answered, "It's simple. I didn't carry a gun."

Previous generations of primate biologists had gone into the mountains carrying large elephant guns because they were frightened of the huge gorillas. The gorillas sensed that these interlopers were scared and probably dangerous. But Schaller, wanting a genuine relationship with the gorillas, entered their jungle without a weapon. Because he was unarmed, he lowered his gaze and moved slowly and deliberately, and the gorillas could sense the care and respect in his approach to them. After a time, seeing he posed no threat to them, they allowed him to sit in their midst and watch all the activities of their family and tribe.[5]

In the same way, you can come to the difficult situations in your life without carrying the weapons of judgment and fear. As you listen quietly and openly, a way through your difficulties will become clear.

It never hurts to think too highly of a person.
They often act the better because of it.

NELSON MANDELA

AT SPIRIT ROCK, years ago, I led a men's retreat with my close colleagues Wes Nisker, Teja Bell, and Robert Hall. In the evenings we held a council where the men were invited into the center of the circle to talk about being fathers and sons or give voice to their struggles around money. They talked about their confusion around sex or what it means to be a man. Many of the men expressed a lack of fellowship and said how rare it was to talk about their personal lives and not focus on business or sports or other more common conversations. The simple listening and acknowledgment by the other men was healing. They were not alone.

On the third day, one man described having a blues radio show in Los Angeles on Sunday nights. He said, "I have a big following inside the prisons. One day I got a letter from an incarcerated man named George Jameson who wrote, 'I'm a regular listener to your show. And I have a request. Could you play some of the early great blues legends like Mississippi John Hurt and Blind Lemon Jefferson on your show?' Then he listed several other blues greats that he'd also like to hear."

The next week, this host went on his radio show and said, "I got a letter from George Jameson. He is obviously a man with a fine understanding of the blues. He's an aficionado of the early masters, and I'm going to play his requests for some Mississippi Delta blues, Muddy Waters, Blind Lemon Jefferson, Mississippi John Hurt, and others."

And then a few weeks later, he got a second letter from George Jameson. George wrote, "Man, I gotta thank you for playing all those blues greats. It was a special show for me. I want you to know that it was the first time in my life I can remember my name being said with respect. Thank you."

A FEW YEARS AGO, I was invited to teach at the British parliament mindfulness group while I was visiting England. Parliament was facing Brexit and other political turmoil, so I led everyone present through a steady heart meditation. Then I invited each member to envision one of the wisest elders of Parliament in past centuries and hear what message that elder had for them in navigating hard times. Winston Churchill came, as did Thomas Cromwell and Queen Elizabeth I, all reminding the members of inspiring leadership of the past. After we practiced, we told each other who came up for us and then opened the room for members to share their thoughts and ideas.

"This is the best thing we do all week," they said, relief in their voices. "When we get quiet, when we meditate, then we can listen to each other, even from different sides of the aisle."

These members of parliament, the labor and the conservative members who were usually at odds, created a way to connect and care. Their mindful listening was a form of respect.

WHILE WALKING THE PATHS of the Oxford University campus in England, viewing the gothic chapels and ancient dining halls, my guide likened the medieval buildings to Harry Potter's Hogwarts. The curated paths and buildings displayed centuries of care and craftsmanship. Then I learned from an environmentalist there that one of the oldest colleges at Oxford, built in the 1500s, used huge oak beams to hold up the ceilings in the dining hall. But after five hundred years, these giant beams had begun to succumb to dry rot, and the caretakers of the college had grown concerned. "You simply can't get enormous five-foot-wide oak beams anymore," they said. "What to do?" Finally, someone suggested they talk to the college foresters.

The foresters said, "We have been waiting for you to contact us." They explained that when the college was built, the builders and foresters anticipated a time, hundreds of years in the future, when the beams would need to be replaced. They planted a special grove of oak trees for this purpose in the Oxford forest preserve. Now, the foresters said, there are five-hundred-year-old oaks ready to become the new beams.

What a thoughtful way to live. To tend our world. To make something beautiful. And in doing so, to plan with vision and respect for the generations of the future.

PRACTICE

Mindful Loving Awareness
with a Bow of Thanks

Loving awareness is Ram Dass's synonym for *mindfulness*. By greeting each experience with loving awareness, we are able to offer respect to whatever arises. In this way, the focus of our meditation isn't about self-improvement or gaining some special experience. It is about bringing the spirit of loving awareness and a respectful heart to it all. We practice simply, letting things settle, noticing when we get entangled, acknowledging it all with kindness, without getting caught in reactions and responses. By releasing our clinging we shift from the creation of suffering to the open space of freedom.

Here is how to meditate with this gracious spirit—offer a thank you to whatever arises!

Start by sitting quietly and invite your body to come to ease. Now, bring a mindful loving attention to your breath. Wherever you feel it, notice the subtle changing rhythms, shallow or deep, soft or slow. Rest with the rhythm of the breath for a time, breath by breath inviting a sense of calm. Then say to your breath, "Thank you. Thank you for breathing so steadily all my life. Thank you for breathing together with the trees and the global ocean of air and all life on earth. Breath, you can relax. I'm OK just here and now. Thank you." Notice the ease that arises as the breath responds to this gracious thank you.

Next, bring a mindful loving awareness to your body. Feel the whole body together, as a field of sensations, vibrations, and energy. Notice the areas of hot and cold, tension and ease, and open to sense the ever-changing field of bodily life. Sense, too, how much your body carries for you, the stress and concerns and love. Hold it with quiet kindness for a minute. Then say to your body, "Thank you. Thank you for holding so much and for continuously sustaining my life. I'm OK just here and now. You can relax. Thank you." Notice what happens as you relax.

Now shift your attention to your heart. Become aware of all the feelings and emotions your heart carries. With mindful loving awareness sense the tears and the love, the longing and the joy, the fear and anger and grief and excitement and tenderness and courage, all that is held in your heart. Hold them kindly. Sense how your loving awareness can hold it all. Rest with this for a minute. Then say, "Thank you. Thank you heart for carrying so much. I'm OK just here and now. You can relax." Notice the ease that comes.

Now, shift your loving attention to your busy mind. Notice its stream of thoughts and images, ideas, plans, and memories. Feel the ever-present moving energy of the mind. As a witness to its constant concerns, honor it all with gratitude and kindness. Take a deep breath. Then say, "Thank you mind. Thank you for working so hard to keep me safe. You can relax. I'm OK just here and now." Let the mind settle and feel the ease increase.

Finally, notice that in observing the body, heart, and mind, you are outside of them. You have become a loving witness of the changing field of body sensations, feelings, and thoughts. These experiences are not who you really are.

Turn back to sense that you are the awareness; you are the consciousness that knows. Consciousness is like space, containing all things but not limited by them. You can say, "Thank you," to conscious awareness itself.

It is amazing to be conscious. Relax into this open space of awareness. Rest in it. It is your home.

Generosity of Vision

Nothing
Will Change,
Unless We Can
Envision It

Holy! Holy! Holy! . . .
Everything is holy! everybody's holy! everywhere is holy!
everyday is in eternity! Everyman's an angel!

ALLEN GINSBERG

THE FOLLOWING STORY, the Vimalakirti Sutra, comes from the Mahayana tradition of India, which developed in the centuries that followed the Buddha. The Mahayana is known for its many sages and bodhisattvas of compassion and for its vast imagination. Both Buddhist and Hindu writings of this era describe how we live amidst multiple universes, boundless and numerous as the grains of sand on the Ganges River multiplied by the same number of grains of sand. While staggering in number, this vision matches the recent revelation of hundreds of billions of galaxies and trillions of stars reported by the Hubble and Webb telescopes.

Consider this story an invitation to expand the range of your imagination and vision. A unique gift of human consciousness is our immense power to envision and create. Look around you. Almost everything you see that is human built, made, created, and employed was first seen in someone's imagination. Imagination holds generosity and creativity and possibility—all forces we need to remember, especially in difficult times. Even now we are being called to envision a wise future and respond with our deepest creativity, our good hearts, and our care for this magnificent earth.

The ability to see this world with a vast perspective is the subject of this story, a debate or competition among spiritual beings—the great monks and sages, the arhats and bodhisattvas, when the Buddha encourages them to visit a layman named Vimalakirti, who is ill. In the hierarchy of the times, the revered monks and bodhisattvas were considered far above the lay people. But like many great texts that open our eyes, this debate turns that idea on its head. The highly esteemed bodhisattvas cling to the rules and perspectives they had been taught, but their diligent service to the teachings blind them to deeper truths that Vimalakirti points them to. Vimalakirti beckons them into the vast power of imagination and the silent openness that holds them all. He calls them, and all of us, to the big task of imagining something much greater for our future. It reads like a magical fairy tale of old.

Once upon a time, in the garden of Ambapali at Vaisali, eight thousand monks and nuns, all of whom were enlightened, gathered at the foot of the Buddha to hear him speak. The enlightened ones were as calm and dignified as royal elephants, and they were surrounded by thirty-two thousand bodhisattvas, spiritual healers from all the great traditions and from all over the world. Sunlight danced above their heads, and the world sparkled with the morning light and the aroma of flowers.

The Buddha, radiant and glittering as he sat high above them to share the Dharma in the beautiful garden, expounded on the teachings of the compassionate heart. And when he was done speaking, the bodhisattva Ratnakara, along with five hundred youths, approached him. Each of them held a parasol made of seven kinds of jewels, and they circled the Buddha with great reverence. Together they lay down their parasols before the Buddha, and when they made this gesture, all the parasols transformed into one single parasol, which became a brilliant canopy so that it formed a covering for a billion galaxies. The surface of the canopy reflected the limitless eternity of all the galaxies and all the suns, moons, and stellar bodies in the universe. This was the vision and power of the Buddha.

Ratnakara then knelt down on the ground, pressed his palms together, and praised the Buddha: "Pure are your eyes and pure is your thought; immeasurable is your virtue. All that the Buddha sees can be seen with the eyes of holiness, can be seen with beauty."

After celebrating the Holy One, Ratnakara then asked the Lord Buddha to explain to the youths the purification of the Buddha field.

"The Buddha field is pure when the mind is pure," the Buddha responded. "This very world is as glorious as any other Buddha world. It is only our defilements that prevent us from correctly seeing it as such.

"Now," he went on, "I want all of you, dear disciples, to go and visit the layperson Vimalakirti. He has grown ill. And he is in need of your care."

Indeed, not far away in the city, the layman Vimalakirti was ill at home. And because it is the task of a bodhisattva to care for those in need, they would do as instructed by the Buddha and offer their care to him. But they were reluctant to go.

"Go on my behalf," said the Buddha. "See what he needs."

Vimalakirti was a layperson, but he was no ordinary man. In fact, he too was an awakened being dedicated to the service and care of all. But he was not a monk or a nun. He was a householder with a wife and a son, and from that place he lived in a very pure manner, with the aim of helping all sentient beings to wake up.

He appeared to be adorned with ornaments, yet he was only endowed with the simple garments of a hermit. He seemed to eat and drink, yet his nourishment really came by the heart of meditation. He entered the everyday world to bring the spirit of love to every corner of the universe. He went into the casinos so he could teach the gamblers about nonattachment. He consorted with politicians to teach them the unused power of truth telling. He wandered into the bordellos so he could teach about sacred connection. Vimalakirti was not afraid to go anywhere.

"Where does he reside?" one bodhisattva asked.

"He sits on the seat of love," the Buddha said. "He exudes the qualities of love and it affects everything he touches. Because he lives with an awakened heart, he plants seeds of goodness everywhere he goes. And because he plants these seeds, miracles happen all around him."

But even with these words, the Buddha's disciples and bodhisattvas were still not thrilled about going to visit Vimalakirti for he had a history of one-upping the bodhisattvas. He played tricks on them and spun crazy wisdom that turned what they knew on its head. They felt challenged by him. Once, many years earlier, the Buddha himself had gotten sick, and Ananda, one of the Buddha's most kindhearted and devoted attendants, decided to get some milk at the market to help him. Ananda went out with his alms bowl, and as he was walking to town, he ran into Vimalakirti.

"Is there anything I can offer you?" Vimalakirti asked.

"Yes, you could give me some milk for the Blessed One," Ananda said.

Vimalakirti looked shocked. "*What* are you doing?" he exclaimed.

So Ananda repeated himself: "I'm out to get milk for the Buddha, who has an illness, and I believe it will help."

Vimalakirti shook his head. "An illness!" he said. "Reverend

Ananda, the body of the Buddha is like diamonds. It's beyond good and evil, beyond sickness. How could disease or discomfort possibly touch such an awakened one? You insult him by going out for milk. You have to understand true liberation is not bound by these small concepts of body and healing and sickness. That's all duality."

Ananda shrank back. "All right, I take your point. It may all be nondual, but what am I to do?" he asked.

Vimalakirti continued, "The Buddha is like the vast sky and the shining stars. How could you get milk for that? You don't understand what you're doing in this world."

Harsh words. Understandably, Ananda felt confused and sad.

The Buddha, in his mind, heard this conversation and said, "Ananda, the householder Vimalakirti speaks to you of deep truth. And yet, nevertheless, since I have appeared in this time as a human being, with the difficulties that humans have, Ananda, do not be ashamed. Go ahead and get me some milk."

The Buddha affirmed both Vimalakirti's teaching and Ananda at the same time. Everyone who witnessed the teaching was called to see reality deeply on another level. But Ananda felt a bit distraught. Thus was the spirit of Vimalakirti. He messed with the sages. He played with their thoughts. He challenged how they viewed the teachings. He teased them until they said, "Okay, I surrender. I see that there's something bigger that I have to pay attention to." So when the Buddha called on the bodhisattvas to go visit Vimalakirti, little did they know, even Vimalakirti's very illness was a trick and a teaching. Vimalakirti had brought on his illness in order to call forth the great enlightened ones. He knew their bodhisattva vow committed them to attend to him in a time of need. By bringing illness to himself, Vimalakirti was making a profound gesture of self-sacrifice. He was willing to embody that which is difficult in order to bring all the healers together and offer the teachings in his heart. He knew that by bringing illness to himself, he would constellate a great outpouring of love. He knew people would rush in from every side to help.

As the bodhisattvas approached the home of Vimalakirti they were hesitant—but also confident. Revered for their mastery of the Dharma, they were convinced they would be the ones teaching Vimalakirti, but when they arrived, they were met with a bright and expansive calm. Despite his illness, Vimalakirti sat in his bed radiating vitality and clarity.

"Where have you been, Vimalakirti?" one disciple asked.

"Well, I've been everywhere. To the hell realms and across all the lands and beyond."

"Well, where should we sit, Vimalakirti?" another disciple, Sariputra, asked. "There are no chairs."

Vimalakirti looked at him and teasing him, said, "Did you come here for the sake of the Dharma, or did you come for the sake of a chair? What are you looking for?"

"The Dharma, of course," said Sariputra.

"Well, where are the best chairs in the great galaxies?" Vimalakirti asked.

"Oh, there is a Buddha who lives in a realm not far from here who has magnificent thrones that are eighty-four thousand feet high, and they're covered with jewels and lotuses and peacock feathers," one disciple responded.

"Well then, let there be chairs!" Vimalakirti exclaimed.

And at that very moment, by his own magic, Vimalakirti

summoned from another distant Buddha field thirty-two thousand vast lion thrones. The seats were so majestic and giant that the bodhisattvas would have to transform their bodies to the size of giants to sit on them.

Vimalakirti's expanded heart made the room inconceivably large, royal, and beautiful, pointing them all directly to the possibility of imagination and to the potential for a generosity of spirit that we all can hold. You may not have something, but if you open your mind and your heart, that alone can make the magic.

"And this is nothing," Vimalakirti said, gesturing to the grandeur of it all. "The liberation of all beings can pour into a single pore of a bodhisattva's skin. All the waters of the four great oceans can pour into a bodhisattva without injuring anything in the water. All the animals such as fish, tortoises, crocodiles, frogs, and other creatures can enter without them even being aware of a problem; the whole transformation is visible without any injury or disturbance to the frogs and the alligators. Such a bodhisattva can reach his right hand and pick up a whole galaxy and open it for you to see and understand and bring illumination to all the beings that are there."

When the bodhisattvas were seated, Vimalakirti went on, explaining his illness in spiritual terms, equating it with the fundamental existential malaise of all sentient beings. But then, as they moved closer to his bedside, he asked them to consider his sick form.

"Am I this sick form? Am I this body? Are you your body? Who are we really?" he asked.

The bodhisattvas all looked very closely—both at him and

at themselves. They tried to rebut or argue with him. But in his presence, it was almost as if there was nothing to argue. They began to see how each of them was far vaster than the body alone. Vimalakirti prompted their imaginations to see that they were not limited by their bodies or their stations. Within them there was something unlimited. Free. Each of them carried an undying spirit that was as vast as the universe.

Vimalakirti then grew silent. He sat still on his bed, his eyes twinkling with wisdom and kindness. After a moment of hesitation, one disciple stepped forward and posed a question: "Vimalakirti, what is the essence of true understanding?"

In response, Vimalakirti reached for a delicate glass jar filled with sand. He held it up for them to see, then gently shook it. The grains danced wildly, swirling in chaotic patterns. The bodhisattvas watched intently, puzzled by his choice of demonstration. After a few moments, Vimalakirti set the jar down and allowed the sand to settle. Gradually, the grains came to rest, forming a smooth surface. He pointed at the calm sand, a serene smile on his face. Intrigued, the bodhisattvas began to ponder the meaning behind his actions. "Just as the sand settles into stillness," Vimalakirti said, "so too can the mind find clarity in silence."

The disciple furrowed his brow, thinking of ways to challenge this lesson. "But how can we help others if we do not speak to them? Is not the sharing the words of the Dharma a path to enlightenment?"

Vimalakirti then gestured toward the open window, where children played in the streets below. Their laughter floated up like music, a reminder of the joy and spontaneity of life. Vimalakirti smiled wider, as if inviting the bodhisattvas to join in the celebration of existence.

"Words are but one way to express our understanding," he seemed to say. "Sometimes, the heart speaks louder in silence than in sound. Compassion and love can flow through presence and action, beyond the confines of language."

The bodhisattvas exchanged glances, touched by the depth of Vimalakirti's teaching. They had come to challenge him but found themselves being challenged instead. One finally spoke up: "But what about the complexities of life? How do we navigate the struggles and suffering of our world without words to guide us?"

Vimalakirti picked up a vibrant flower from a vase nearby, holding it delicately between his fingers. He admired its beauty, allowing the monks to observe the intricate patterns of its petals. Then, he placed the flower back and closed his eyes, entering a moment of profound stillness. The bodhisattvas watched, captivated by his sheer presence. In that silence, they felt a wave of peace wash over them, a reminder of the beauty and possibility that exists everywhere. The worries of their minds began to fade, replaced by a deep sense of connection to the world around them. Inspired by his wisdom, the bodhisattvas realized that the silence they had sought to break was, in fact, a bridge to deeper understanding. Enlightenment, they understood, was not a destination but a timeless way of being. It is found in the simplicity of presence, in every flower, here in any single moment. The enlightened beings thanked Vimalakirti.

"You've made our life more fully awakened and bearable," they said. "We will do what we can to protect you."

Vimalakirti, complete with his teachings, then picked up

the entire assembly in his room in one hand and transported them all back to the Amrapali garden to sit with the Buddha once again.

❊

Vimalakirti's teachings remind us that when we see rightly, the leaves on the trees become like pages in the holy books. You don't have to look any further than where you are to see that all is sacred and mysterious. Who you are is not limited to your body, and you're not limited by the conditioning of your culture or your family. You don't have to limit your imagination with these small stories. You can sense something so much greater and more magnificent about yourself and this world and see it everywhere you look.

Expand your ways of moving through this mysterious life. Imagine a new possibility—like the single jeweled parasol that turned into a canopy that held billions of sparking galaxies. Come and help those who are in need. And always remember to sit on the seat of love.

What can I say that I have not said before?
So I'll say it again.
The leaf has a song in it.
Stone is the face of patience.
Inside the river there is an unfinishable story
    and you are somewhere in it
and it will never end until all ends.

Take your busy heart to the art museum and the
    chamber of commerce
but take it also to the forest.
The song you heard singing in the leaf when you
    were a child
is singing still.
I am of years lived, so far, seventy-four,
and the leaf is singing still.

                MARY OLIVER[1]

SOME YEARS AGO, I stood at the top of Mount Tamalpais at noon. The planet Venus was in transit across the face of the sun, and a number of people had brought their biggest telescopes to view the spectacle.

I was invited to look through one of the large telescopes—and the moment I looked through the lens, I was transported. I saw the golden ball of the sun with its roiling surface and fiery plumes, and then there was Venus—a whole planet the size of our earth, looking tiny compared to the sun, just a dark round marble that slowly moved across the broad face of our great glowing star.

As I gazed at these distant orbs, I felt how I too was on a sister planet, circling around the sun, taking a ride. I sensed that I was standing on a planet, tiny compared to the vastness of our star, dancing amidst the breadth of the whole solar system. And I surrendered to this invitation to vastness, to eternity.

As a kid, I used to love to lie down on the grass and gaze up on a starry night. It was exhilarating to look at the stars. Then I started to imagine that I was stuck like a magnet on the bottom of the earth, held to the earth by the force of gravity. I felt as though I was looking downward into a great sea of stars. It gave me a rush of excitement, imagining I was on the verge of falling down into it.

Here we are held on our little blue-green globe, circling our star amidst vastness and mystery.

Wisdom comes when we see with a vast
    perspective.
Our life is unfolding in the timeless galaxies.
We turn with the stars in cycles of light and dark,
birth and death, joy and sorrow.
Surrounded by vast peace.

Sometimes I go about in pity for myself,
and all the while a great wind
carries me across the sky.

OJIBWA SAYING

HERE IS ANOTHER PART of the Vimalakirti Sutra, a playful and profound account that turns the ancient patriarchy on its head. In this version from Rick Fields, we see how our modern work to uplift women and honor their enlightenment has actually been understood for millennia.

>Once the Buddha was walking along the
>forest path in the Oak Grove at Ojai, walking without
>arriving anywhere
>or having any thought of arriving or not arriving
>
>and lotuses shining with the morning dew
>miraculously appeared under every step
>soft as silk beneath the toes of the Buddha
>
>When suddenly, out of the turquoise sky,
>dancing in front of his half-shut inward-looking
>eyes, shimmering like a rainbow
>or a spider's web
>transparent as the dew on a lotus flower,
>
>—The Goddess appeared quivering
>like a hummingbird in the air before him
>
>She, for she surely was a she
>as the Buddha could clearly see
>with his eye of discriminating awareness wisdom,

was mostly red in color
though when the light shifted
she flashed like a rainbow.

She was naked except
for the usual flower ornaments
Goddesses wear

Her long hair
was deep blue, her two eyes fathomless pits of space
and her third eye a bloodshot
ring of fire.

The Buddha folded his hands together
and greeted the Goddess thus:

"O Goddess, why are you blocking my path?
Before I saw you I was happily going nowhere.
Now I'm not sure where to go."

"You can go around me,"
said the Goddess, twirling on her heels like a bird
darting away,
but just a little way away,
"or you can come after me.
This is my forest too,
You can't pretend I'm not here."

With that the Buddha sat
supple as a snake
solid as a rock
beneath a Bo tree
that sprang full-leaved
to shade him.

"Perhaps we should have a chat,"
he said.
"After years of arduous practice
at the time of the morning star
I penetrated reality, and now..."

"Not so fast, Buddha," the Goddess said,
I *am* reality."

The earth stood still,
the oceans paused,
the wind itself listened
—a thousand arhats, bodhisattvas, & dakinis
magically appeared to hear
what would happen in the conversation.

"I know I take my life in my hands,"
said the Buddha.
"But I am known as the Fearless One
—so here goes."

And he and the Goddess
without further words
exchanged glances.

Light rays like sunbeams
shot forth
so bright that even
Sariputra, the All-Seeing One,
had to turn away.

And then they exchanged thoughts
and the illumination
was as bright as a diamond candle.

And then they exchanged mind

And there was a great silence
as vast as the universe
that contains everything

And then they exchanged bodies

And clothes

And the Buddha arose
as the Goddess
and the Goddess
arose as the Buddha

and so on back and forth
for a hundred thousand
hundred thousand kalpas.

If you meet the Buddha
you meet the Goddess,
If you meet the Goddess
you meet the Buddha.

Not only that. This:
The Buddha is the Goddess,
the Goddess is the Buddha.

And not only that. This:
The Buddha is emptiness
the Goddess is bliss,
the Goddess is emptiness
the Buddha is bliss.

And that is what
and what-not you are
It's true.
...
Bliss is emptiness
Emptiness is bliss
Be your breath, Ah
Smile, Hey
And relax, Ho

And remember this: You can't miss.

Anything a man can do, I can do.

DIPA MA BARUA

IN 1989, AT AN INTERNATIONAL Buddhist teacher meeting with the Dalai Lama, we Western teachers brought up how often unworthiness, self-criticism, shame, and self-hatred arose in Western students' practice. The Dalai Lama and other Asian teachers with him were shocked. They could not quite comprehend the concept of self-hatred. There is no such word in Tibetan. It took the Dalai Lama some time conferring with Geshe Thupten Jinpa, his wonderful translator, to understand it. Then he turned and asked if many of us experienced this problem in ourselves. He saw nods of affirmation from all of us. He seemed genuinely surprised.

Then he got quiet and tender, almost tearful. Gazing at us, he responded, "But that is mistake," he said. "Every being is precious!"

I certainly knew how to hide self-judgment, suffering, and shame in myself. In order to survive the many years of physical violence and abuse within my family, I covered over my pain. I became a peacemaker and a good boy. When my parents were battling, I tried to calm them down—without much success. When I went to school, I tried to stay safe by pleasing the teachers. Secretly I envied the "bad boys"—the ones who skipped class, smoked behind the school, and got into trouble. It looked like they were having more fun. Today, of course, I know that many of them were struggling too, acting cool to deal with their own fears.

While trying to be good, underneath I carried a feeling of being unlovable, of forever seeking acceptance. In meditation I got to know the painful and empty feelings more consciously. I learned to put my hands on my belly and heart to hold the pain and emptiness. My mother tells me that as a baby, I cried and cried. My twin brother and I, and my next brother, born a year later, were all allies in survival for most of our childhood, while my parents were triply overwhelmed. For me, the baby bottle I got on a rigid schedule with while my parents fought, it seems, was not enough to make me feel loved. Outwardly my life seemed fine. Inside I felt a hole in my heart and with it a sense of being unlovable. It took time, but gradually through meditation and therapy and healing, I learned to find inner nourishment, acceptance, and love. Now, while I can remember that pain, it seems to have belonged to another incarnation. Yes, I still have pain and troubles like all human beings, but it is not who I am. I am joyful and free.

Each of us has our own measure of pain. Sometimes the pain we suffer is great and obvious; sometimes it is subtle. Compassion and self-love can transform it. When you hold your life with tenderness and courage, a shift of identity occurs, a shift to a sense of being whole. By kindly embracing your brokenness, you can make a loving return to your original unshakable goodness.[3]

ANANDA, THE BELOVED attendant of the Buddha, was sent by the Buddha on a mission. On that hot day, he passed by a well near a village, and seeing Pakati, a young woman, he asked her for water to drink. Pakati said, "O monk, I am too humbly born to give you water to drink, lest your holiness be contaminated, for I am of low caste." And Ananda replied kindly, "I asked not for caste but for water." The young woman's heart leaped joyfully, and she gave Ananda a drink.

Ananda kindly thanked her and went on his way, but she followed him at a distance. Having heard that Ananda was a disciple of Gautama Shakyamuni, the young woman went to the Blessed One and cried, "Please help me, and let me live in the place where Ananda your disciple dwells, so that I may see him and minister to him, for I love Ananda."

The Blessed One understood the emotions of her heart, and he said, "Pakati, your heart is full of love, but you do not understand your own sentiments. It is not Ananda you love, but his kindness. Accept then his kindness and practice it with others. With this kindness, Pakati, you can become a model for noble men and women. Follow the path of justice and righteousness, and you will outshine the royal glory of queens on the throne."[4]

WHEN WE SENSE that we are all worthy, our hearts know that we are part of the same family. Expand your imagination. Our neighbors, our countrymen, even our politicians are all our uncles and aunties, our wacky grandparents, our brothers and sisters. We take care of our families. We've all heard the story of the many Danes who wore Jewish stars when the Nazis required it of Jews. And we need to remember how we belong to each other.

In August 2016, a couple named Cari and Lauri Ryding came home to find that the rainbow flag that had flown on their front porch had been stolen and their house egged. Antihomosexual vandalism wasn't at all what they expected in their close-knit Massachusetts neighborhood.

As it turned out, it also wasn't what their neighbors expected. As Dennis Gaughan, one of the neighbors, explained to the *Boston Globe*, "We said, 'Why don't we all have the flags? They can't take them from all of us.'" Within days, the rainbow flag—the symbol of gay pride—was flying in solidarity with the Rydings on over 40 other homes in this family-friendly area. "One person's act of fear and maliciousness created a powerful statement of love.... Love wins!" said Lauri.[5]

ROBERT DESNOS, a celebrated French poet who joined the resistance during the Nazi occupation, worked underground for many years until he was captured and sent to a concentration camp. One day, he and other resistance fighters in the camp were gathered up and forced into the back of a big truck. They all knew they were headed for the gas chamber.

When the truck stopped, a commander ordered them to file out of the truck. People were tired and emaciated. Facing death, they were bewildered, shocked, and terrified.

Desnos pushed his way to the front of the line, grabbed the hand of the man first in line, looked at it with concentration, then told the man that he had a very long lifeline.

You can imagine the confusion at this moment.

Desnos, positively exuberant, went on to tell the man that he was going to have three more children. He then grabbed another man's hand and read their palm and spoke about all the good things that were going to happen to him as well. Then he did this with another person. And another. And another.

The guards were slack-jawed. Who was this guy at the front of the line reading palms? Desnos went on and on, and soon everybody—including the guards—was smiling.

This is not what was expected. Everyone had thought that the resistance fighters were going to their death. Now even the guards were so confused they were unable to go through with the executions. When Desnos had finished reading everyone's palms, including the guards', the guards told everyone to get back in the truck. They were all going back to the barracks. Not one person from that truck ended up headed to that gas chamber.[6]

Maybe when we're in trouble we should do something crazy and unexpected and it will help us. We can use our imagination as a force to save us. Even in difficult times, the most deplorable of circumstances, it's possible to sense beyond the moment and create something much bigger. Take the roof off, blow the clouds away, and see the stars.

Despair is a failure of imagination.

WADE DAVIS

We inhabit, in ordinary daylight, a future that was unimaginably dark a few decades ago, when people found the end of the world easier to envision than the impending changes in everyday roles, thoughts, practices that not even the wildest science fiction anticipated. Perhaps we should not have adjusted to it so easily. It would be better if we were astonished every day.

REBECCA SOLNIT

DR. SANJAY GUPTA, a celebrated physician who regularly appears on CNN, had always wanted to meditate with the Dalai Lama. So an early morning meeting was arranged at the Dalai Lama's private residence in Dharamsala. Before the doctor met with the Dalai Lama, the staff gave him a protocol to follow. He was told that the Dalai Lama would be sitting in his meditation room and that the doctor should walk in quietly and make his bow and then sit in the place that had been set up for him next to the Dalai Lama. Afterward, the doctor could talk about the experience.

Dr. Gupta opened the door and walked into a modest room where the Dalai Lama was already meditating. Dr. Gupta joined him and as he sat there quietly, all of his meditation insecurities began to kick in. He tried to meditate. Time passed. And after a while he heard the Dalai Lama's deep, distinctive voice say, "Any questions?"

Dr. Gupta then looked up and saw the Dalai Lama's smiling face as it began to break into his characteristic laugh.

"This is hard," Dr. Gupta said.

"Me too!" the Dalai Lama exclaimed. "After doing daily for 60 years, it is still hard!"

This was at once surprising and reassuring for the doctor. Who knew that the Dalai Lama, the great Buddhist spiritual leader, also had trouble meditating? But perhaps it is not the meditation itself that is hard for him, but the responsibilities he carries. His heart holds the immense suffering of the oppressed Tibetan people and his care for the many sufferings of the world.

Then the Dalai Lama gave Dr. Gupta some instructions. He suggested that Dr. Gupta focus on a problem he was trying to solve, rather than a traditional object of meditation focus, like the breath. He told Dr. Gupta to separate the problem or issue from everything else by placing it in a large, clear bubble. Dr. Gupta did as he was instructed. Then, as he placed the physical embodiment of the issue into the bubble, something happened. The problem was now floating right in front of Dr. Gupta. In his mind, he could play with it, flip it, and rotate it. As the bubble moved around, it was also freeing for him. He felt less attached to emotions, to other ideas, and to other associations. In other words, the problem isolated itself and came into a clear-eyed view.[7]

Even though the Dalai Lama holds the suffering in the world, he also remains joyful and kind. This same clear-eyed view and joy in the midst of it all is what we so desperately need in the world today.

A STRANGER WALKED toward the gates of a new city. By the side of the road sat an old wise woman who hailed the traveler: "Welcome!"

"What kind of people are they who live here?" the traveler asked her.

"How did you find them in the home city you left?" asked the wise woman.

"They were gossips, mean-spirited, and often selfish. Difficult to get along with."

"You'll find the people of this city to be likewise."

Later, a second stranger passed by and was welcomed by the old woman.

"What kind of people are they who live here?" the second traveler asked.

"How did you find them in your home city?" asked the old woman.

"They were fine people—industrious, open-minded, and easy to get along with."

"You'll find the people of this city to be likewise."

SOME YEARS AGO, THE BBC AIRED a special show on the sixtieth anniversary of the end of the Siege of Leningrad. During World War II in 1941, Leningrad was besieged by the German army, cut off for almost three years and three long Russian winters.

Hundreds of thousands of people were close to starving. The BBC interviewed an older woman who had lived through this time of enormous hunger and cold as a child. She said that in the biting cold, she went out to pick up her weekly ration of bread for her and her mother. She stood in the long bread line on a street that was slippery with ice and finally went in to receive their piece of bread. As she came out, she fell on the ice and the bread fell into a mud puddle. She was young, she said, maybe seven, and she sat there and wept. The woman who walked out behind her reached down and helped her up. Then she carefully tore her own week's piece of bread in half and wrapped it in a cloth and handed it to her.

After she spoke, the old woman beckoned the BBC camera crew to follow her down the hallway of her railroad-type apartment into the kitchen. She opened a cabinet. There was a special covered ceramic bowl from which she pulled out a blue kerchief. She untied it, and inside it was the piece of bread. She had saved it for all those years. She explained that that woman's bread gave her the heart to live through the years of the siege and the war, and that she would never forget it.

> Imagination is the only weapon
> in the war against reality.
>
> LEWIS CARROLL

YEARS AGO, during Occupy Wall Street, members of the East Bay Meditation Center (EBMC) in Oakland, California, went out to demonstrate. They were concerned about the inequalities of our current financial system, so they held their protest right in the center of the city, in front of a number of the big banks.

As the Occupy crowd grew, the banks locked their doors, while the bankers secured themselves inside to continue with their work. But like all banks, many of the walls were glass. The bankers could see the demonstrators outside, and the demonstrators could see the bank workers inside. Instead of exhibiting anger, the EBMC demonstration created a different kind of statement. They rounded up a big stack of one dollar bills and stood just outside the door of one of the biggest banks in Oakland. Instead of taking money, with a bow, they handed free money to everybody who walked up.

ON FOURTH STREET, in the center of Louisville, Kentucky, there's a public monument to a mystical experience. It celebrates a moment when Thomas Merton, who had spent years as a Christian contemplative, was walking down the street on an errand for his monastery. In that spot, quite suddenly, he had a revelation: every single person who passed him was shining like the sun. "I was suddenly overwhelmed with the realization that I loved all those people, that they were mine and I theirs, that we could not be alien to one another even though we were total strangers," he wrote. "There is no way of telling people that they are all walking around shining like the sun."

Usually, historic markers denote places of historic battles, places where hundreds were killed. But this marker calls us to remember that a visionary experience is possible for all of us. It is possible to see the holy everywhere and in everyone. Merton wrote, "The only problem with seeing this was that I wanted to fall down and worship every single person who went by."[8]

For years Merton had been making prayers in the monastery, looking for what is holy. Then it appeared like grace, walking down the shopping street in Louisville on an ordinary day.

RICHARD SELZER, a surgeon at Yale University, described the mystery of love after performing a surgery:

> I stand by the bed where a young woman lies, her face postoperative, her mouth twisted in palsy, clownish. A tiny twig of the facial nerve, the one to the muscles of her mouth, has been severed. She will be thus from now on. As her surgeon I had followed with religious fervor the curve of her flesh; I promise you that. Nevertheless, to remove the tumor in her cheek, I had to cut the little nerve. Her young husband is in the room. He stands on the opposite side of the bed and together they seem to dwell in the evening lamplight, isolated from me, private. Who are they, I ask myself, he and this wry mouth I have made, who gaze at and touch each other so generously, greedily?
>
> The young woman speaks. "Will my mouth always be like this?" she asks. "Yes," I say, "it will. It is because the nerve was cut." She nods and is silent. But the young man smiles. "I like it," he says. "It is kind of cute." All at once I know who he is. In ancient Greece the gods appeared as mortals. I understand and I lower my gaze. One is not bold in an encounter with a god. Unmindful of my presence he bends to kiss her crooked mouth and I so close I can see how he twists his own lips to accommodate to hers, to show her that their kiss still works. And I hold my breath to let the wonder in.[9]

ZEN TEACHER Karlfried Graf Durckheim instructs us all, "Do not turn away":

> The first necessity is that we should have the courage to face life and encounter all that is most perilous in the world. The aim of Zen practice is not to develop an attitude which allows a person to acquire a state of harmony and peace wherein nothing can ever trouble him. On the contrary, practice should teach him to welcome the demons, to let himself be assaulted, perturbed, moved, insulted, broke and battered—that is to say, it should enable him to dare to let go his futile hankering after harmony, an ease of pain, and a comfortable life in order to discover, in doing battle with the forces of struggle, that which awaits him beyond the world of opposites.
>
> Thus when the person who, being truly on the Way, falls upon hard times in the world will not, as a consequence, turn to that friend who offers him refuge and comfort and encourages his old self to survive. Rather, he will seek out someone who will faithfully and inexorably help him to risk himself, so that he may endure the suffering and pass courageously through it. Only to the extent that a person exposes himself willingly over and over again to annihilation, can that which is indestructible arise within him. In this lies the dignity of daring.[10]

VEDRAN SMAILOVIĆ LIVED in the ancient and storied city of Sarajevo, which was battered in the Balkan War between Bosnia and Serbia in the 1990s. For three years, the beautiful city he loved was besieged by violence. People lived among mortar fire and rockets. No one could get in, and no one could get out, except for a few United Nations helicopters. And those who tried to escape were often killed by mortar fire.

Smailović was a cellist in the Sarajevo Philharmonic Orchestra. During the siege, he would dress in his tux, grab his folding chair, and go out to wherever the mortars had struck to play his cello. People waited for him to appear. He played in ruined buildings, amidst the threat of snipers, and during funerals. In one stretch he played Albinoni's Adagio in G Minor for twenty-two days in a bomb crater in a ruined square of a Sarajavo marketplace to commemorate the twenty-two people who had been killed there. He played magnificent music every day so that the people of the city would not forget their beauty and would not give up hope.[11]

A man is running hard
to catch the bus that just left.
It's picking up speed but he
pulls even and raps on its side,
and a woman by the window
yells to the driver, who stops
and opens the accordion door.
But the man does not get on—
he points back to an old woman
who has not run a step
in a very long time
shuffling towards the bus.
Nor does he leave until he's
helped her up both steps
then walks back slowly
still breathing hard
toward us who are
waiting for a different bus.
What can a group of strangers
do at a time like this?
A time in its own tiny way like
when Bob Hayes roared by them all
to bring the relay home,
or when Billy Mills devoured

the last 50 of the 10,000 meters
or when Joan Benoit came striding
into the stadium alone—
and all of us
strangers stood up and cheered.

LASZLO SLOMOVITS[12]

A NUMBER OF YEARS AGO, the Menninger Foundation sponsored a conference on consciousness at which Mad Bear, an Iroquois medicine man, spoke. After several days of discussion and meetings and the presentation of scientific papers, it was his turn. "For my presentation I'd like us to begin by going outside," he said.

We followed him out into a big open field where he asked all present to stand silently in a circle. For a while we stood in silence under the wide-open sky, surrounded by vast fields of grain stretching out to the horizon. Mad Bear then began to speak, first by offering a prayer of gratitude. He thanked the earthworms for aerating the soil so that plants can grow. He thanked the grasses that cover the earth for keeping the dust from blowing, for cushioning our steps, and for showing our eyes the greenness and beauty of their life. He thanked the wind for bringing rain, for cleaning the air, for giving us the life breath that connects us with all other beings. He went on thanking everything around us for a long time. We stood in this circle for nearly an hour. I found myself both inspired and, at times, slightly tired and bored. But eventually I surrendered and listened, and together our mindful hearts grew quiet with him and became one with each prayer. We felt the prairie's wind on our faces and the packed earth beneath our feet. We saw the swaying movements of grass and scudding clouds anew. In Mad Bear's presence, all was received with a reverent sense of connectedness, gratitude, and love.

This is spiritual practice: love infusing our awareness, enabling us to openheartedly accept the gift of each moment.[13]

I TREASURE MARY OLIVER'S inspiration that in the end we might say that I was a bride married to amazement.

OVER MANY YEARS, my wife Trudy and I traveled to help lead retreats with Ram Dass. The year before he passed, he was eighty-seven and in a wheelchair.

That whole week, Ram Dass taught love. In fact, he almost always taught love. He said to us, to everyone, "I love everything. I love you and you and you. I love the whole group. Every single one of you and your children and your parents, however they treated you. I still love them."

At his home, which was his temple, a statue of Kwan Yin and pictures of the Buddha, Mother Mary, his guru Neem Karoli Baba, Gandhi, and a hundred other saintly figures—all the usual suspects—sat on his big altar. In the middle he had an image of Donald Trump. (It had been Dick Cheney, but he had switched it out.) He loved them too. During the retreat, he spoke of how he loved the walls and the ceilings and the lights and even the shoes that everyone had taken off and left just beyond the practice space. "I love this dirty carpet," he said.

Hearing this, one of his students took a piece of that dirty carpet, put it in a gold frame, and sent it to him, challenging him to put it on his altar, which he did, right next to his guru.

At one point, a friend asked, "Are you in much pain these days?" She knew the answer was yes. He had been in a wheelchair for twenty years, unable to move half of his body. He had lived through infections and sores and illnesses. She asked him out of a kind courtesy.

"Yes, my feet hurt," he said.

"And how about your arms, your legs?" she asked.

"Yes, they hurt, too," he said.

"And do you have pain in your back?"

"Oh yes," he responded.

And then he paused for a minute. He smiled the most amazing smile.

"I love my pain," he said, just like he was saying, "I love everything."

You are not your body. This body is not you. You can honor the body and love it and care for it. But you are not limited by this body. You are life without boundaries. You are the eternal play of consciousness itself. You have never been born and you have never died. Look at the sky and the ocean filled with stars since before time. Say, I am them. I have always been. I am free. Birth and death are only doors through which our spirits pass, thresholds on our journey. Birth and death are a game of hide and seek. Come and hold my hand. We'll meet again and again in this dance.[14]

THICH NHAT HANH

RECENTLY, I READ OF A MAN who wanted to volunteer at a large, local homeless mission. He said that due to COVID concerns, he was not allowed to serve in person. Instead, the mission asked if he could provide the ingredients for a meal for 600! The man took it as a challenge and enlisted the help of his children. They drove from store to store looking for huge quantities of food from the list, including 101 eight-ounce cans of green beans and boxes of pasta, pounds of ground beef, gallons of iced tea, and six hundred breadsticks! They managed to get everything they needed for a warm meal on a cold winter night. It was an adventure! The family turned it into a game, and it was joyful. Doing this didn't just provide a meal, it taught the man's whole family what being a cheerful giver really means.

TWELVE-YEAR-OLD MATHEW FLORES from Sandy, Utah, approached postal worker Ron Lynch and asked if he had any extra advertisements or random newsletters. The boy explained that he loved to read but couldn't afford books or even the bus fare to the library, so he would take anything the mailman had. Lynch was floored. "He didn't want electronics; he didn't want to sit in front of the TV playing games all day. The kid just wanted to read," Lynch told *Deseret News*. Lynch asked his Facebook friends for reading material. Soon, Flores was getting books from all over the world—the United States, England, and even India. For his part, Flores said that he plans to read all the books, then share them with other book-starved kids.[15]

We cannot do great things. But we can do small things with great love.

MOTHER TERESA

PRACTICE

Vast Imagination and the Altar of Love

Vimalakirti invites us to sit under a canopy of bejeweled umbrellas, vast as the cosmos. He shows us that our imagination is big enough to contain everything.

Ram Dass's spreading altar brings this to life. With a hundred images of saints, sages, and occasional sinners too, we are welcomed into the vastness of the awakened heart.

This whole world is our temple. Let us envision transforming it into a world that's not ruled by greed or hatred or fear. Let us envision the creation of a world without injustice and inequality and racism and the dangers of climate change. So much is possible.

We have mind-bending outer technology. Who would've imagined that you could have the great library of Alexandria in your pocket along with a hundred million cat videos?

It is time for the outer developments of technology to be matched by the inner development of humanity. The world only changes when we envision the transformation we wish to see. The task for us is to imagine another way and shepherd it into being.

❊

Begin by allowing yourself to sit quietly.
Take a few long breaths and settle your mind and heart.

Invite your mind and heart to fill with lovingkindness and compassion.

Imagine like Ram Dass's altar that your consciousness spreads out across the whole glorious and troubled world, holding it all kindly and tenderly. Then place it all on a huge table of love.

Practice directing the power of compassion and lovingkindness: Envision the sick children in hospitals across the world and feel your heart of compassion deepen. Envision all the weary healers, the nurses and doctors caring for them, and let the heart of sympathy and appreciation for healers across the world grow vast. Sense your wish to support them.

Now, imagine the many hungry and frightened children in war zones across the world. Let the compassion grow vast. Now envision the peace workers and aid workers and caring parents and community members striving to help and hold these children and let the appreciation grow deep as well. Sense your wish to help them.

Imagine the endangered orangutans in their last forest preserves, the endangered polar bears on ice floes. Let your connection and sympathy grow vast. Now picture the scientists and biologists and all those working to protect and save these magnificent beings and their habitats. Send them your loving support.

Open your consciousness to the countless acts of goodness and care happening just now across this globe. Simple acts. People stopping at red lights so the others can drive safely. The millions of parents making breakfasts of rice gruel and tacos and eggs and oatmeal for their children every morning. People working in offices, teaching one another, serving one another, tending their homes and villages and communities.

As vast as your mind and heart are, so is this ongoing ocean of human kindness. Sense the earth enveloped in it.

Bring to mind the places of struggle and suffering, picture the conflicts in Europe, Africa, the Middle East, the US. Imagine all those who live there, caught in the pain of fear and power struggles. See them breathing more easily. Picture peaceful resolution, under the umbrella of care and compromise. Sense how much you wish for this.

Now imagine this force of goodness spreading and touching the hearts of the leaders of the world, enveloping those who are struggling and those who are causing suffering.

Send them all wishes of lovingkindness. Say to them, "May you be free from hatred. May you be free from fear. May you be free from delusion. May you remember the reality of love."

Imagine you are surrounding the world with a field of kindness and the shining force of love. This force can gradually awaken the hearts of beings everywhere and turn the direction of humanity toward unshakable compassion and kindness.

Finally, see the world as your temple. When you go to the marketplace, imagine all exchanges as a blessing of love. Each time you pass a school, let yourself see it as a shrine of wisdom. Pass along goodness to new generations and send your blessings.

When you engage in business, no matter what others do, let it be a joyful exchange based on love. Everywhere, like Vimalakirti, plant seeds of goodness and care. It is with the power of this vision that we can create a world filled with blessings.

Healing and Freedom

The Power
of the Listening
Heart

Love heals. Heals and liberates. I use the word *love*, not meaning sentimentality, but a condition so strong that it may be that which holds the stars in their heavenly positions and that which causes the blood to flow orderly in our veins.

MAYA ANGELOU

IN THE STORY THAT FOLLOWS, Dr. Richard Selzer, a writer-surgeon, reminds us of the mystery that connects us. He shares a beautiful account of the celebrated Tibetan doctor Yeshi Dhonden that speaks to the tender relationship between medicine and the human experience. Some years ago, I had the chance to be with Yeshi Dhonden when I was dealing with a neurological problem. I had received an inaccurate diagnosis, one that was quite dire, so I went round see him. He cast a gentle gaze toward me as he scanned my body and took my vitals, and in his warm presence I was reassured. He said, "You don't have to worry about this. Just take these little pills and you will be fine." They looked like rabbit poop, to be honest. They were dark little Tibetan medicine remedies. "Also do these meditations," he said. "It will be all okay."

I felt much better just being with him. I felt held and received and respected as a human being. Beyond the pills and the meditations, the gift of his presence was perhaps the most healing thing.

All of us want to be received like this.

In Yeshi Dhonden we can sense the power of the listening heart, of caring in the face of suffering, illness, and death. This is the healing force we need in our world. Can we listen to the pulse of one another? Can we listen to the pulse of the world?

※

On the bulletin board, in the front hall of the hospital where I work at Yale, appeared an announcement. "Yeshi Dhonden" it read, "will make rounds at six o'clock on June 10th." The particulars were then given, followed by a notation: "Yeshi Dhonden is personal physician to the Dalai Lama." I'm not so leathery a skeptic that I would knowingly ignore an emissary from the gods. Not only might such sangfroid be inimical to one's earthly well-being, but it could take care of eternity as well. Thus, on the morning of June 10, I joined the clutch of white coats waiting in the small conference room adjacent to the ward selected for the rounds. The air in the room is heavy with ill-concealed dubiety and suspicion of bamboozlement. At precisely 6:00, he materializes—a short, golden, "barrelly" man dressed in a sleeveless robe of saffron and maroon. His scalp is shaven, and the only visible hair is a scant black line above each hooded eye.

He bows in greeting while his young interpreter makes the introduction. Yeshi Dhonden, we are told, will examine a patient selected by a member of the staff. The diagnosis is as unknown to Yeshi Dhonden as it is to us. The examination of the patient will take place in our presence, after which we will reconvene in the conference room where Yeshi Dhonden will discuss the case. We are further informed that for the past two hours Dhonden has purified himself by bathing, fasting, and prayer. I, having breakfasted well, performed only the most desultory of ablutions, and given no thought at all to my soul, glance furtively at my fellows. Suddenly, we seem a soiled, uncouth lot.

The patient had been awakened early and told that she was to be examined by a foreign doctor and had been asked to produce a fresh specimen of urine, so when we entered her room, the woman showed no surprise. She had long ago taken on that mixture of compliance and resignation to the facies of chronic illness. This was to be but another in an endless series of tests and examinations. Yeshi Dhonden steps to the bedside while the rest stand apart, watching. For a long time he gazes at the woman, favoring no part of her body with his eyes but seeming to fix his glance at a place just above her supine form. I, too, study her. No physical sign or obvious symptom gives a clue to the nature of her disease.

At last he takes her hand, raising it in both of his own. Now he bends over the bed in a kind of crouching stance, his head drawn down into the collar of his robe. His eyes are closed as he feels for her pulse. In a moment he has found the spot, and for the next half hour he remains thus, suspended above the patient like some exotic golden bird with folded wings, holding the pulse of the woman beneath his fingers, cradling her hand in his. All the power of the man seems to have been drawn down into this one purpose. It is the palpation of the pulse raised to the state of ritual. From the foot of the bed where I stand, it is as though he and the patient have entered a special place of isolation, of apartness, about which a vacancy hovers and across which no violation is possible. After a moment the woman rests back upon her pillow. From time to time, she raises her head to look at the strange figure above her, then sinks back once more. I cannot see their hands joined in a correspondence that is exclusive, intimate, his fingertips receiving the voice of her sick body through the rhythm and throb she offers at her wrist. All at once I am envious—not of him, not of Yeshi Dhonden for his gift of beauty and holiness, but of her. I want to be held like that. Touched so, *received*. And I know that I, who have palpated a hundred thousand pulses, have not felt a single one.

At last Yeshi Dhonden straightens, gently places the woman's hand upon the bed, and steps back. The interpreter produces a small wooden bowl and two sticks. Yeshi Dhonden pours a portion of the urine specimen into the bowl, and proceeds to whip the liquid with the two sticks. This he does for several minutes until a foam is raised. Then, bowing above the bowl, he inhales the odor three times. He sets down the bowl and turns to leave. All this while, he has not uttered a single word. As he nears the door, the woman raises her head and calls out to him in a voice at once urgent and serene. "Thank you doctor," she says, and touches with her other hand the place he had held on her wrist, as though to recapture something that had visited there. Yeshi Dhonden turns back for a moment to gaze at her, then steps into the corridor. Rounds are at an end.

We are seated once more in the conference room. Yeshi Dhonden speaks now for the first time, in soft Tibetan sounds I've never heard before. He has barely begun when the young interpreter begins to translate, the two voices continuing in tandem—a bilingual fugue, the one chasing the other. It is like the chanting of monks. He speaks of winds coursing through the body of the woman, currents that break against barriers, eddying. These vortices are in his blood, he says. The last spendings of an imperfect heart. Between the chambers of the heart, long, long before she was born, a wind had come and blown open a deep gate that must never be opened. Through it charge the full waters of her river, as the mountain stream cascades in the springtime, battering, knocking loose the land, and flooding her breath. Thus he speaks, and is silent.

"May we have the diagnosis?" a professor asks.

The host of these rounds, the one man who knows, answers.

"Congenital heart disease," he says, "Interventricular septal defect, with resultant heart failure." A gateway in the heart,

I think. That must not be opened. Through it charge the full waters that flood her breath. So! Here then is the doctor listening to the sounds of the body to which the rest of us are deaf. He is more than doctor. He is priest.

I know...I know...the doctor to the gods is pure knowledge, pure healing. The doctor to man stumbles, must often wound; his patient must die, as must he.

Now and then it happens, as I make my own rounds, that I hear the sounds of his voice, like an ancient Buddhist prayer, its meaning long since forgotten, only the music remaining. Then a jubilation possesses me, and I feel myself touched by something divine.[1]

A FEW YEARS AGO, I sat with a woman who was going through multiple rounds of chemotherapy. She had advanced metastatic cancer and the medicine had been very painful for her. She said the chemo was like a fire moving through her body. It burned. She felt as if she was in hell.

So the next time she had to do a round of medicine, I stayed with her and held her hand. I invited her to close her eyes. I asked her to imagine that that medicine traveling through her veins was purifying her. "Let it lead your body to a transformed well-being and a restored spirit," I told her. I encouraged her to visualize her body as a great healing temple and the fire as an offering as it burned through.

"Yes, I can feel the fire," she said. "When I feel it as something purifying, it comes surrounded by a beautiful green light and a lovely spirit. This is exactly what I need for my body."

No longer was she resisting it.

Though the chemo had understandably been terribly painful and frightening, she allowed herself to get closer to it. She did not resist her body; she was now attending her body with loving awareness.

Loving awareness allows us to trust our bodies and open our hearts to hold this human incarnation with its tainted glory, beauty, and pain. Healing can come when we turn toward our struggles with our whole hearts and listen deeply to a reality beyond our fears.

DURING WARTIME in Southeast Asia, I visited a Vietnamese temple that was founded by a special visionary whom they called "the coconut monk." He lived primarily on coconuts and his home was on a dedicated "island of peace." Because he was known as a peacemaker, I wanted to learn from him and his community.

I traveled to see him on a boat through the Mekong Delta during a period of a lot of fighting. Helicopter gunships and firefights were there on the horizon. And yet amidst the war, life continued. Some people were shopping; others were farming. Despite the violence, people kept doing all the things needed to keep their life going because they were human beings. We all still have to live.

When the boat pulled up to the dock, I went directly into the temple. There, monks from several countries were all wearing robes with a big patch on them that displayed an assault rifle broken in half and lettering that said, "We will fight no more." Their temple was a sanctuary, a refuge in the middle of the war. It was a place where young men who didn't want to enter the battles could come. Instead, they could become monks in order to make peace. They were courageous and strong. I paid my respects, then wandered out into the open air.

At the far end of this island, there was a hill. And on that hill stood a statue of a standing Buddha, thirty feet above everything. Just next to him was a thirty-foot statue of Jesus. They had their arms around each other's shoulders. High above them, and far out to the horizon, you could still see the helicopters and battle. But not here on the island. It was as if those two statues stood there to say, "Hey, we're brothers in love; there's another way to live in this world than what you see out there."

Both the Buddha and Jesus were known as great healers—healers of body, of heart, and of spirit. On the island they stood tall to remind us to heal and to share that healing love with everyone we meet.

> We all carry within us our places of exile,
> our crimes, our ravages. Our task is not to
> unleash them on the world; it is to transform
> them in ourselves and in others.

ALBERT CAMUS

WE ARE NOT LIMITED by our age. We are not too young nor too old. Think of what Greta Thunberg did at fifteen, and what Toni Morrison and Jimmy Carter did in their seventies and eighties. Whatever age, we can touch others with our free spirit and our presence by being fully alive. The man in this next story shows us how it's done:

I'm ninety-two years old, all right. I get up every morning at 7:00 am. Each day I remind myself, "Wake up, get up!" I talk to my legs, "Legs get moving. Legs, you're an antelope." It's a matter of mind over matter. You have to have the right spirit. And I'm out on the streets, 7:30 am sharp.

I'm wearing my Honorable Sanitation Commissioner badge they gave me from City Hall. I'm alert. I'm ready, I'm out there. And I got my whistle. My job is I help get parked cars off the street so they can bring in the sanitation trucks and the Wayne Broom, the big one—thirty grand for a broom! So when they show up, I go around blowing my whistle to get people to move their cars. I have a great time.

People are asleep. They're busy with business. They're busy taking time off from the business. They're busy having a good time. Whatever. I don't care. I blow my whistle. I'm all over the place.

I don't discriminate, either. I go after the sanitation men too. The union got them a coffee break. Some coffee. They're having eggs, they're having bacon, they're having toast . . . they're having French toast. I kid them about it. And I go right into the restaurant and blow my whistle. They love it, they understand. Everybody loves it, everybody understands. It's the whistle that gets them. Sometimes I'm having such a laugh, I can't blow it. Then I get back to work. "Schleppers, get moving, let's go!"

This used to be a beautiful city. People cared. If you didn't pay your rent, the sheriff would come and put your furniture out on the street. But the poorest of the poor would come automatically and drop their pennies and nickels at your house and put you back into your apartment. That's neighborhood.

Now it's different. Things have gotten out of kilter—hard to say why. People seem to be lost in their own lives. I see them on the street, lost in their own thoughts. Not that I'm all that different. I'm a schlep myself. I have as many bad habits as anyone. You should see my apartment. It's a mess. Me, Mr. Clean! But I'm trying. Let's try. It's all possible.

What can I tell you? I'm not a saint or a wise man. I'm not the 2000 Year Old Man. I'm only the ninety-two-year-old man. Just a senior citizen. But what do I know that everybody doesn't know? We know. I just go out there in the morning and blow my whistle. That's what I do. You do what you do. Me, I'm having a great time. Wonderful fun. And when people see how much fun I'm having, they have to laugh. What else can they do? And then I hit them with it: "Move your car!"[2]

I learned that opening myself to my own love and to life's tough loveliness not only was the most delicious, amazing thing on earth but also was quantum. It would radiate out to a cold, hungry world. Beautiful moments heal, as do real cocoa, Pete Seeger, a walk on old fire roads.

ANNE LAMOTT

Ordinarily I go to the woods alone, with not a single friend, for they are all smilers and talkers and therefore unsuitable.

I don't really want to be witnessed talking to the catbirds or hugging the old black oak tree. I have my ways of praying, as you no doubt have yours.

Besides, when I am alone I can become invisible. I can sit on the top of a dune as motionless as an uprise of weeds, until the foxes run by unconcerned. I can hear the almost unhearable sound of the roses singing.

❀

If you have ever gone to the woods with me, I must love you very much.

MARY OLIVER[3]

WHEN THE HEART IS KIND, everything changes. Nearly two thousand years ago, in the deserts of Egypt and Sinai, among communities of Christian desert fathers, there were mystics and meditators. One was a beloved elder named Abbot Anastasius. One day a young man came and asked if he could join the order and be with the brothers who were part of the abbot's community. Immediately the young man was welcomed in and given a robe and a place to live.

There in the chapel, the abbot kept a beautiful Bible inscribed with gold leaf and exquisite calligraphy, which was used every day in their evening services. The young man, who had been very poor, coveted it, so one night he made off with it and ran away to the city.

The young man went into the market to find a shop that dealt with books and antiquities. At the antiquarian shop, he rang the bell, and when the shopkeeper stepped forward, he said, "I have a special book, and I'd like to sell it to you."

"Ah yes, please show it to me," the shopkeeper said.

The young man brought out the bejeweled Bible, which held both the New and Old Testaments. The merchant knew about these things and when he looked at it, he said, "Leave it with me for a day or two, and I'll tell you what it's worth."

"I'd like to get eighteen gold coins for it," he said. It was a big number.

"Just leave it," the merchant said.

Two days later, the young man went back furtively, found the merchant, and said, "I've asked for a great deal of money, because I believe it's a beautiful book. Will you not give it to me?"

"Yes, I've discovered it is worth exactly as you said," the merchant said.

"How do you know that?"

"Well, I went out in the desert to see my friend Abbot Anastasius, who knows about such things," the merchant replied. "And I showed him this beautiful book and he said, 'Oh yes, it's very valuable, easily worth eighteen gold coins.'"

The young man held his head down in shame. "Did he say nothing else?" he asked, his voice faint and troubled.

"No, not another word," the merchant said.

Then the young man began to weep. He said, "Oh, I've forgotten something really valuable. I need to return this book!" And then he ran all the way back to the community. There he dropped to his knees and wept and begged to the holy abbot and said, "I misunderstood what was really the treasure in this place. I took the wrong thing. Here is your beautiful book. Can I come back?"

"You can keep it if you like," the Abbot responded kindly. "If it means that much to you."

"No, no, I can't keep it!" the young man said. "If I keep it my life will never be happy. I was mistaken to take it. Can I come back?"

The abbot agreed. Grateful, the young man became a monk and lived in the community as a loving member for all his years thereafter.

WHEN MY TEACHER Ajahn Chah first came to visit the US, he had an old image in his head of what he would see. The images he carried came from watching old Hollywood movies—deserts and cowboy Westerns, and big buidlings with urban dramas. We picked him up at Logan Airport in Boston, then escorted him into a big van with the other monks who had traveled with him. From there, we headed out toward central Massachusetts where the countryside becomes rural.

On the way we drove down Memorial Drive and showed him the most famous places. "Here's MIT and here are the towers of Harvard and here is the renowned Mass General Hospital."

Then we got on the Massachusetts Turnpike and drove twenty minutes until we were finally out of the city. We began to pass fields and woods. New England has a lot of forests. And as we drove along, Ajahn Chah's eyes got bigger and bigger. "What are these woods?" he exclaimed. "What are these forests? Pull over. Pull over!"

We pulled over and he hopped out of the van and walked up to the fence at the edge of the turnpike. In every direction, all you could see were pine trees and maples and oaks. His eyes remained wide.

"Wow!" he exclaimed. "Who lives in this forest?" He was smelling it. Taking it all in. "What kind of animals live in this forest?" he asked. "Do you have bears? Deer? Are there mountain lions who live in here?"

After a minute he turned to me and said, "How far do these forests go?"

"Oh, they stretch more than a thousand miles north up toward the Arctic," I said. "They go a really long way."

He got very excited. Forget Harvard and MIT. He was a forest monk. He wanted to know the Western trees and the natural world surrounding it all. Trees offer a healing that universities can't touch. I told him we were going to a meditation center surrounded by forest and trees. He looked immensely happy.

From the start of the Buddhist tradition, trees have played a huge role. The Buddha was born under a tree. He practiced his meditation under a tree. He got enlightened under the Bodhi tree. He taught under the great Indian trees for years. And he died resting beneath two beautiful Sal trees, which burst into flowers. He taught that trees and nature are a gateway to a calm, open mind.

A few years before this visit, I had visited another Thai forest master, Ven. "Buddhadasa," I told him, "often students in America have trouble with self-compassion. There's a great deal of self-judgment and criticism, shame, and trauma. Do you have any advice for us?"

"Yes, it's simple," he said. "Take them out into the woods. Have them spend time with the trees and the rivers. Bring them into the natural world and teach them the meditations of lovingkindness. After they've been out there for a while, they'll get better."

As soon as healing takes place,
go out and heal somebody else.

MAYA ANGELOU

DON JUAN IS SAID to have told Carlos Castaneda that the most difficult part of the sorcerer's way is to realize that the world is a feeling.

This is a mysterious statement.

The healing gift of loving awareness is that we can begin to know the domain of our feelings. Loving awareness helps us not to be afraid of anger or grief, envy and loneliness, or even joy. Some people are so loyal to their suffering that they're afraid of feeling joy. They don't know how to dance with their feelings.

C. S. Lewis said, "For the first time I examined myself with a seriously practical purpose. And there I found what appalled me; a zoo of lusts, a bedlam of ambitions, a nursery of fears, a harem of fondled hatreds."[4] Of course there is also an ocean of joy, a meadow of tenderness, and a mountain of delight and caring. True healing and liberation come when we expand the window of tolerance so we can bear the fullness of our humanity. Without that, we are tossed around, like a boat without a rudder.

Make a healing space by listening to the emotions and longings of your own heart; hold your own psyche with loving awareness. Be patient, and let love take its time. It is this capacity of steady awareness that allowed Nelson Mandela to transform the suffering of twenty-seven years in prison and come out with enough magnanimity and compassion to transform South Africa. It is this steady love that allowed Nobel laureate Wangari Maathai to establish a nationwide movement to plant fifty-one million trees in Kenya. Even though she was put in prison, in founding the Green Belt Movement, she inspired a nation.

The human realm is one of ten thousand joys and ten thousand sorrows. No need to take these human feelings so personally. You're going to have them all, but they don't define you. When you learn to let them come and go, they become the free energy of life itself.

THE ONLY THING that binds you is your own mind.

The Buddha explains:

> Who is your enemy? Mind is your enemy.
> No one can harm you as much as your own mind, untrained.
> Who is your friend? Mind is your friend.
> No one can help you more than your own mind well trained, not even your parents, your children, or the most loving partner.[5]

Heaven knows we need never be ashamed of our tears, for they are rain upon the blinding dust of earth, overlying our hard hearts. I was better after I had cried, than before—more sorry, more aware of my own ingratitude, more gentle.

CHARLES DICKENS

MANY YEARS AGO, two Russian astronauts were stranded in space. Their space vehicle broke down and their capsule didn't work right. There was a very good chance that they weren't going to make it back.

Eventually they somehow corrected what was needed and began a rather precarious return, complete with a fiery descent. When they landed in Kazakhstan, the first thing they did as they exited their space capsule was to get down on their knees and kiss the earth.

In space they had looked down at the earth with so much longing. They were grateful to simply return to this planet and their human life.

You have a human life, just like theirs. And you have just as much reason to rejoice in it. You can either get lost in the past and future, lost in busyness and worry, or with loving awareness, you can honor your tears and joys and stay present for all of it.

Let yourself be tender with the world. It's your world. The world is your lover in a way that nothing else is. It's always here. You can go out right now and kiss the earth.

Overcome any bitterness that may have come because you were not up to the magnitude of pain entrusted to you. Like the mother of the world who carries the pain of the world in her heart, each one of us is part of her heart, and therefore endowed with certain measure of that cosmic pain. You are sharing in the totality of that pain. You are called upon to meet it in joy instead of self-pity.

PIR VILAYAT INAYAT KHAN

RACHEL NAOMI REMEN, a beloved physician who uses art, meditation, and other spiritual practices in the healing of cancer patients, tells a moving story that illustrates the process of healing the heart as well as the body. She describes a young man who was twenty-four years old when he came to her after one of his legs had been amputated at the hip in order to save his life from bone cancer. When she began her work with him, he had a great sense of injustice and a hatred for all "healthy" people. It seemed bitterly unfair to him that he had suffered this terrible loss so early in his life. His grief and rage were so great that it took several years of continuous work for him to begin to come out of himself and to heal. He had to heal not simply his body, but also his broken heart and wounded spirit.

He worked hard and deeply, telling his story, painting it, meditating, bringing his entire life into awareness. As he slowly healed, he developed a profound compassion for others in similar situations. He began to visit people in the hospital who had also suffered severe physical losses. On one occasion, he told his physician that he had visited a young singer who was so depressed about the loss of her breasts that she would not even look at him. The nurses had the radio playing, probably hoping to cheer her up. It was a hot day, and the young man had come in running shorts. Finally, desperate to get her attention, he unstrapped his artificial leg and began dancing around the room on his one leg, snapping his fingers to the music. She looked at him in amazement, and then she burst out laughing and said, "Man, if you can dance, I can sing."

When this young man first began healing with Dr. Remen, he made a crayon sketch of his own body in the form of a vase with a deep black crack running through it. He drew the crack over and over and over, grinding his teeth with rage. Several years later, to encourage him to complete his process, Dr. Remen showed him his early pictures again. He saw the vase and said, "Oh, this one isn't finished." When she suggested that he finish it, he did. He ran his finger along the crack, saying, "You see here, this is where the light comes through." With a yellow crayon, he drew light streaming through the crack into the body of the vase and said, "Our hearts can grow strong at the broken places."[6]

IN INDIA, A MERCHANT FAMILY had a young son they loved very much. At age ten he became seriously ill and fell into a long coma. A number of doctors came to treat the boy but nothing they did could rouse him. Then the parents heard that a celebrated yogi was visiting the village nearby, and they begged him to come and help their son. The yogi came and chanted his most powerful prayers and mantras, but to no effect. Finally he told the parents the only last hope for healing was to offer what is traditionally called an act of truth.

After sitting quietly, the yogi stood next to the boy, took his hand, and confessed that although he was a well-known mendicant, he was in fact a fraud and didn't believe in much of what he taught. At this, the boy opened his eyes and looked around. Now it was the mother's turn. She gazed at her son and said that she had never really loved the father. It was an arranged marriage and though they made a family together, she was never really happy. At this, the boy sat up. All were astonished.

Finally, the boy looked to the father, who reluctantly reflected and then spoke. "Everyone thinks I am a successful merchant, but in fact though I work hard, my business is almost bankrupt and I have not let my creditors know that they may not get paid," he said. At this the boy stood up, was quite well again, and hugged his mother and his father.

Through these acts of truth, the boy was healed and the family began again. They looked anew at each other, now willing to tell the truth, and a fresh tenderness and compassion was born.[7]

I HAVE HELPED LEAD retreats for veterans, some who saw combat in the wars in Iraq and Afghanistan. These vets often feel isolated even from their own families. They carry a weight on their souls and say things like "I can't really share my story—I can't tell you what I saw," and worse, "I can't tell you what I had to do."

At the retreats we created a safe community, often the first place they felt they could tell their stories—the ones they hadn't told anyone since their return. In this protected space, when they shared the burdens of their hearts, and when they listened to the stories of combat vets, a remarkable healing happened. They were no longer shut off, silently traumatized, alone. They begin to heal and return, in body and soul.

My beloved wife, Trudy, created the same healing field when she helped build a program for nurses and medical workers from the local neonatal intensive care unit at Children's Hospital in Santa Monica, California. The nurses shared what they carried in their hearts. Though they experienced great joy in their jobs, they also had to deal with tremendous sorrow. In the neonatal intensive care unit (NICU), some babies thrive and others die. Nurses and doctors who tend and love the babies who die then have to tell parents, "I'm so sorry; your child did not make it." In the NICU, this happens regularly. But there is no time to mourn. As soon as a child is lost, they have to clear out the incubator and get ready for the next baby. The nurses who work at the NICU hold these stories close. They cannot go home and talk over dinner about babies who have died. And yet... sharing with others is a necessary part of all our healing.

At the InsightLA NICU retreat, these nurses told their stories and shared what they carried. It became a sacred space for them to sit quietly and listen from the heart to one another. This tender and respectful practice allowed them to hold each other with the same love they had for their tiny babies.

You can do this too. Invite a few dear best friends. Light a candle. Make a sacred space to talk about what your heart holds. Allow yourself to hold in compassion all the stories that those in the circle share, space for the healing of their own heart.

As Barry Lopez said, "Sometimes a person needs a story more than food to stay alive. That is why we put these stories in each other's memories. This is how people care for themselves."[8] Sometimes we need to hear it and sometimes we need to tell it.

WHETHER MARK TWAIN said this or not, we all can relate: "My life has been filled with terrible misfortunes, most of which never happened."

The fearful mind makes up stories that haven't even happened yet. And yet the same mind can tell stories of love, triumph, and redemption. You get to choose. Choose well.

WHEN JERRY BROWN was the governor of California, I had the pleasure of sitting with him at a dinner honoring one of our mutual friends, and I asked him what he was going to do next, as he was retiring. He had already accomplished many wonderful things. He said, "Well, I'm dropping out of politics, but I am still concerned about two things. One is climate change." And then a grave look came across his face. "And the other thing I'm concerned about is nuclear weapons. There are fourteen thousand nuclear warheads around the world, all in different places. We are two minutes to midnight on the doomsday clock. And I don't know how best to overcome this."

I reflected and then said, "I have a story for you. It may be helpful." I proceeded to tell him a wild story of creation of the universe from Indian cosmology. In ancient India, it was understood that the gods continuously create the world. Brahma is the creator God, Vishnu the sustainer, and Shiva the destroyer. This is the heart of the Hindu pantheon. Universes get created for a billion eons, and then they dissolve, and then new ones are created out of nothing. That's how it works. Everything is created out of nothing. And then it disappears into nothing. Kind of like how the Y2K computer bug disappeared into the void. And your morning's breakfast. Life appears and then it disappears.

In the process of creation there are always both gods and demons. There's a balance of good and evil, joy and sorrow, light and dark, and birth and death. It's duality that creates life. If you have birth, you have death. Everything has its opposite. And in the universe of this story, the gods and demons were enacting their eternal conflict, and in the end the demons were winning. The gods had tried everything, but the demons had more power and were overcoming all the benevolent efforts of the gods. Finally, one of the chief gods said, "We've done all that we can. Our last resort is to call Durga."

Durga is a powerful goddess, the protective mother of the universe, both fierce and loving. Hearing their prayers, Durga arose out of the Himalayan mountains, huge and with many arms, each carrying a weapon. These were her righteous skillful means. She asked the gods what they needed. They explained that their powers were not enough to overcome the demons. She smiled, said, "Not a problem," and turned right toward the demons. In a few days, she subdued their destructive energy. She transformed their fire to save the world.

Then I said to Jerry, "Maybe all the men who have been working to limit these nuclear weapons and all the men who've been trying to stop their proliferation are unable to do so. They don't have the power or the answer. What this story tells us is that maybe it's time to call in the mothers. Maybe it's time for the mothers and the grandmothers to come out. To stand up, to speak fierce truth, to help transform the fire. Maybe the feminine energy of life can save us in a way that men haven't been able to do."

WE CAN BE LIMITED or liberated by our stories, the personal and the collective. Healing comes when we can step back and ask ourselves, *What are the stories we use to define ourselves and our society?* Then we can reflect and choose the beneficial direction. As the Dalai Lama says, "Some of these stories do not have my best interest in mind."

BENEATH ALL THE STORIES, listen to your body. Begin with silent loving awareness, the vastness that is your true nature. Then, listen carefully to your body, and it will tell you what it needs. Next, step back and listen to your mind without getting lost in it. Offer it respect and careful attention, not judgment. Make the space for loving awareness to say, *Oh yes, this is my conditioning. These are the thoughts that have repeated. This is what I've learned. This is what appears. This is healthy. And this is not so helpful because my heart knows things that my mind can't know.*

In the stillness, your heart knows what's healthy and what's wise in ways that you can't think of.

There is in all things an inexhaustible sweetness and purity, a silence that is a fountain of action and of joy. It rises up in wordless gentleness and flows out to me from the unseen roots of all created being.

THOMAS MERTON

REMEMBER READING *SIDDHARTHA* by Hermann Hesse in high school? After his time as a renunciate, Siddhartha had a great love affair with Kamala. During his wandering final years, he ended up sitting by the river and listening to all the different voices in its movement. He heard the joyous voice and the sorrowful voice, the lament of those who yearn and the laughter of the wise. Finally, he allowed all the voices in the river to pass through him. He didn't bind himself to any thought or feeling. He didn't get caught in one perspective nor get lost in any of the different voices.

All of a sudden he heard it all as a great harmony. He felt at peace, sensing the harmony that says, *You can live in this world in a different way.* You can let the voices move through you and be at peace. And because this world holds your family, because it's your earth, because it's your children, you can still act. Not because you're angry at anybody but because you know better. You can reach out and mend the places that need mending; you can stand up for justice, but with your heart at peace. Every action can come from a place of love. Love is the great power to make a difference in this world.

A BEAR PACED UP AND DOWN the twenty-foot length of its cage for fifteen years. When the cage was removed, the bear was given a bigger place to roam, but he continued to pace back and forth the length of twenty feet as if the cage was still there.

Like the bear, you can live in a conditioned way, guided by a small sense of self, following your usual thoughts, your patterns, and the limited ways you define yourself. But this is not who you are. Here's a practical way you can understand this: When you look in the mirror, you will notice how you've aged. You've got some wrinkles here and there—or some extra skin. Your hair thins; your body droops. But the remarkable thing is you don't necessarily feel older!

That's because it's only your body that's aged. You are born with an infant body and then you have the body of small child, then an adolescent, then a young adult, then you are older, and then it starts to fall apart. And you notice, "Oh, I don't feel older!" That's because your consciousness is not limited to your aging body. Beyond your body, you are that same bear—but roaming free.

When you look in the mirror, you become the conscious witness of your body. In not feeling older, you sense that this changing body is not who you are, that you are more than the body and all the identities you've been carrying. You are the consciousness that was born into your body and that will leave at the mysterious moment of death. When it happens, you will see this truth so clearly.

You don't have to be limited like the pacing bear. Even now, you can step back, shift your identity, and become a quiet witness to life. You are not the body; you are consciousness. You have space to choose. Compassion and freedom are your natural abode. You can always rest in this loving awareness.

AFTER HIS INITIAL YEARS of ardent and dedicated practice in the Lao and Thai mountains and jungles, my teacher, Ajahn Chah, went to see Ajahn Mun, the greatest forest master of the era. Seeking guidance, he described all his meditation experiences. He told of lights, visions, and deep insights.

His master looked at him and said, "Chah, you missed the point! Those are just experiences. They're like movies: a war movie and a romantic comedy, a documentary and a history movie. Meditation states, like all things in life, come and go. The most important question is *to whom do they happen?* Who is witnessing or seeing all this?"

Turn your attention from the movies of your life back toward the awareness itself. Become the One Who Knows. *This* is your gateway to healing and to freedom.

BUDDHIST TEXTS OFTEN BEGIN with phrases like "Oh nobly born." They remind you of your original nobility, that you are the child of the awakened ones. You are born with a fundamental dignity and nobility that no one can take from you.

The deepest healing takes place when you remember this. You are fundamentally free. This revelation brings what Siddhartha called the laughter of the wise. Human incarnation is a dance. We suffer at times, it's true. We love and we must also let go. With wisdom, we can do all of this from a place of compassion and freedom. Rather than holding on to the changing seasons of life, we can see it as a play and rest in the place of witnessing, of loving awareness.

Freedom isn't found in the Himalayas or Zen temples or wherever you can imagine it to be. There's only one place where it can be found and that is within your own heart.

You are consciousness; experience it as loving awareness. Rest in this great heart of love not because you're supposed to but because it's your home.

WITH LOVING AWARENESS, notice how you approach this human body. In unhelpful ways, you can judge it, use it, worry about it, or compare it to how you want it to look or feel. You can live with bodily anxiety, or you can disassociate from it and just go about your business and not care about your body at all. A lot of people choose dissociation, or as James Joyce described in *Dubliners*, "Mr. Duffy lived a short distance from his body." Many of us live lives out of touch with our bodies.

But there is a more compassionate and life-affirming approach. Instead of judging or ignoring, you can bring mindful loving awareness to your body. In meditation, you can attend to your body with an open heart. Remember: The point of meditation isn't to become a good meditator. It's to become present, loving, and wise in your own life.

Begin this practice with your own body. When you sit in meditation, the invitation is to be with and listen to your body and learn from it. You'll notice it is a mine field of sensations of warm and cool, pleasure and pain, stress and ease. Your body will show itself to you. And as you sit, you can begin to notice that when you resist the pain and contract around it, the pain will last longer and you will suffer more. Then you can notice what happens if you receive the stress and pain in your body with loving awareness and say yes to this too.

When my grandson was three months old, I did some diaper changes and caretaking. Periodically he cried. He was a baby, and crying is part of their language. But he also cried because he was human. We all cry. Sometimes after he was fed and diapered, he still cried. Then what else could I do? I held him. I offered him a sense of holding and bodily care. And after a while, he settled down.

This kind of holding is the loving care our bodies often need. It is not weakness; it takes courage. Tend to your body just as you would hold a crying child. Bring that same loving awareness to this body, to the hurt, to the tension that you carry because as you go through the day your jaw tightens, and your shoulders get tight, and your back hurts. Sometimes when you sit in meditation and get very quiet and easeful, your body can still hurt. It's not because you are meditating wrong. It's just your body talking. Your body is saying, *Hey, remember me? You've tightened up. I've been holding a lot. Now it's time for all this to begin to release itself.* When you bring a loving awareness, the body gradually opens; it heals itself in a deep way.

Reflect for a moment . . . How do you hold your own body? Do you hold it with worry or longing or love? There's something beautiful and pure about bringing attention to this body without judgment.

It's not always easy. Our whole culture sells you on how your body should look. The magazine covers are done with just the right light, just the right makeup, and then the images are airbrushed and Photoshopped. "Look like this," they say. "Here is the ideal."

And then, when we look in the mirror, we think, *I don't look like that; something is wrong with me. I'm the wrong size. My thighs are too thin or my hair is too thick or what's left of it isn't in the right place.* Our culture teaches us to judge our body rather than to love it. Dieting and exercising can become oppressive rather than caring acts.

Here is a radical act: say to yourself, *Healing and well-being take place when I bring a love to my body. To the painful parts and to that which is joyful and beautiful. My body is an instrument to experience the amazing wonder of living.*

When you bring this caring attention into the body, the body can feel it, and it says back, *Thank you, you remembered me. You care for me.* Love your life, your body, just as it is! This is a gate to liberation. You can live your everyday life with mindful loving awareness.

❊

Loving awareness is also required for healing the body of the earth. Your body isn't separate from the earth. The air you breathe crossed the Pacific Ocean, dusted Mauna Loa and the Fukushima Nuclear Power Plant. The water that you drink carries particles drifting in from India, Mexico, and Los Angeles. We continuously co-breathe with the dolphins and the rainforest, the kelp and the ants. We are completely interwoven.

And it gets even weirder. The breath that you're breathing in the space you are sitting in right now is shared with the breath of everyone sitting near you, with everyone who sat in that space before you, and with everyone who will sit in the space after you. It's very intimate. Some might call it creepy. The fact is: We are in this together.

The whole sense of separateness is false. It's not your body; it's the earth's body. To pay attention to your own physical body brings healing, and it spreads caring and healing to the earth.

PRACTICE

The Temple of Healing Meditation

We all need healing. Sometimes we need healing for physical illness. At other times, we need to heal the traumas that we've suffered and the past difficulties we still carry in our bodies. We need release from the struggles and emotions brought about by our conflicts and the pain we experience from the follies of humanity.

To genuinely heal we cannot reject our illness and grief or use anger and aversion to try to get rid of what ails us. Instead, we have to bring a tender, healing energy to all that is sick, torn, broken, or lost. In the Buddhist prayer of healing, we recite, "May I be the healing medicine for those who are sick, for myself and all others." We understand that healing is possible and dedicate ourselves to being part of that healing. We become tender and wise with ourselves and those around us, especially when we are experiencing our own fear and grief.

Sometimes this is all that healing asks: that we become present. Never underestimate your power to heal when you step toward difficulty with courage and love, when you touch pain with healing rather than fear. Our healing comes out of our own kind attention and the kind embrace of another. In this precious life, may you bring this care to the healing of your heart and body.

Here is a visualization to access the inner healing temple (some people visualize easily—for those of you who don't, play with this in your own way):

Sit comfortably and allow your eyes to close. Make sure your seat allows you to be present, awake, grounded, and relaxed. As you sit at ease, feel your connection to the earth. Center yourself and feel how your breath breathes itself in your body. Then, without trying to change anything, bring a kind attention to what's comfortable and uncomfortable in your body. Notice if there's tension, contraction, or pain in certain areas and ease and relaxation in others. Notice if there's clutter in your mind or repetitive thoughts. Notice the state of your heart. Does it feel contracted or soft and open? Is it full of some emotion or feeling, such as fatigue or joy, sadness or irritation? Simply kindly witness whatever is present with loving awareness, without resistance or judgment. Breathe and be easy with it all.

After a few minutes, begin a visualization. Try to envision or sense in any way you can that you are floating up into the air as if on a magic carpet, up into the cool, clear, blue sky. Take your time. Feel or imagine or sense that you're floating above the earth in the stillness of the clear air and luminous sunlight.

After a minute or two, allow yourself to gradually descend. Set an intention to descend into a sacred and beautiful Temple of Healing, a place of great wisdom and healing and love. Let this temple be a surprise. It may be some place you've been before, or it may be some place you've never seen. It may be indoors or out. Come to rest in it. Take as much time as you need to imagine and feel and picture this temple.

Now sense yourself resting in this Temple of Healing. What does the energy of this healing place feel like to you? How does it affect your body and spirit to be present there?

As you sense yourself in this temple let yourself become aware of whatever wounds you carry that require healing. Once you have at least one injury clearly in mind, become aware that there is a beautiful altar of healing nearby. Now imagine yourself sitting in front of this altar. After a time, picture or imagine, any way you can, that a wise and loving healer who lives at this temple is walking toward you. Let yourself be open to, sense, or envision whatever form of luminous being wants to appear. As this healer approaches you, they will bow lightly to you. Next, simply sit together, and they will put their gentle, healing hand on the part of your body where you are most deeply wounded. Feel the presence of this healing hand on your injured limb, your pained heart, or your wounded brow. If you wish, you can take your own hand and put it on the location of your deepest wound. Hold the place of your sorrow, your difficulty, or your illness. Touch it as if joining your hand with this great healing being. Know that no matter how many times you have buried or resisted this injury or sorrow, how many times you've greeted it with fear or aversion, now is the time you can finally open to it.

As you feel your body opening to this healing touch, explore your sensations. Is the touch warm or cool, hard or soft? Let your awareness be gentle, as if learning the loving touch of Kwan Yin, the goddess of compassion, or Mother Mary or Jesus. Feel your wounds, fears, and difficulties touched by pure sweetness and openness.

As the very core of your wound opens to the touch of healing, sense how you've closed off from this pain, how you've wished it would go away, how you've rejected your feelings.

Now you are ready to open your heart to experience this pain at last, held by loving attention, with the touch of this luminous being together with your own hand. Feel the medicine of healing enter you through this touch. Stay with this healing for as long as is helpful. Then shift to any other areas that ask for healing. Take your time.

After this luminous being removes their hand, they have gifts to give you. There is a package of the perfect medicine for you on the altar. This luminous being now places it in your hands. This symbolic medicine will be in the form of a specific symbol of exactly what you need for healing. Open this gift of medicine and see what is inside the box. If you cannot see it clearly, hold it up to the light. It can be anything—glasses, a jewel, a knife, a flower, or a treasure. Hold this symbol of the medicine that you need in your hands and become aware of just what it means for you. Realize that you can know.

Relax and drink in the blessings of being at this healing temple and in the presence of this luminous and wise being. Finally, imagine that they lean over to you with great compassion and whisper into your ear the healing words you most need to hear. Let yourself hear, imagine, think of, or sense the healing words this being offers you. Receive their blessings in whatever way you can. Take these gifts and these healing words with you in your heart. Before you leave, if you have any questions for this wise healer, you can ask them and they will answer you. When you feel complete, simply rest in this temple and allow its healing and compassionate spirit to fill your heart and body and mind. Let it touch every part of your being. Stay as long as you wish.

When you are ready to leave, offer a bow to this healing being with gratitude for everything they've given to you. Even as you depart, know that this temple is inside of you. It is available to return to any time you need it. Remember that you carry all the medicine and healing you will ever need inside your own heart.

To Serve and to Care

Skillful Service
and a Loving Heart

I slept and dreamt that life was joy.
I awoke and saw that life was service.
I acted and behold, service was joy.

RABINDRANATH TAGORE

HAPPINESS COMES WHEN WE live a meaningful life. Meaning comes alive in relation to life itself and to one another. Whether you make art or write, whether you tend other people or tend to a garden, if you can share your dignity, your understanding, your integrity, your vision, and your friendship, your life becomes blessed. It is a precious gift to be of service and an endless source of happiness. It's partly why we do meditation. In some way, meditation practice helps us become present enough that we can live in this way, so we may give our gifts wherever we are, as we are. In this section, we will look at what it means to be of service in this world, to respond to what is needed, exactly as we are.

The tale that follows is an adaptation of Leo Tolstoy's short story "The Three Questions" written in 1903.[1]

❀

One day it occurred to a certain empress that if she only knew the answer to these three questions, she would never stray in any matter: What is the best time to do each thing? Who are the most important people to work with? What is the most important thing to be doing at all times?

The empress issued a decree through the land saying she wanted answers to these questions and that those who knew the answers should come to her palace to receive a great reward. All kinds of people flooded in. The appeal of a reward tempted many.

In reply to the first question—What is the best time to do each thing?—one person advised that the empress should make a really good and detailed calendar. "You should get everything on your calendar and set aside time for all the things that matter," they said.

And another said, "No, you can't really plan everything out on a calendar because life is too unpredictable, and you just have to set aside your amusements and be really present for whatever is calling your attention as it arises."

Someone else said, "Empress, you can't do this on your own. You need a committee, a community of wise people, a council to tell you when to do everything, and you need to follow their advice."

Then someone insisted, "No, you can't consult a committee. You need to consult the magicians and soothsayers. They'll tell you what's coming, and then you'll know exactly what to do."

The responses to the second question—Who are the most important people to work with?—also lacked a certain accord. One person told the empress to place all her trust in the advisors and administrators around her. Others said that she should work with the physicians and the healers. And still others advised that she put her faith in her warriors.

The third question—What's the most important thing to do?—drew another set of equally different answers. Some said science was the most important pursuit; others said religion. Another group claimed that military skills were absolutely the most important thing to practice.

The empress was not pleased. These answers didn't really satisfy her, so she did not give a reward to anyone.

After some time of reflection, she resolved to visit an old woman who lived in a hermitage in the mountains. She was said to be wise, maybe even enlightened. The empress wanted to know if she could answer these three pressing questions. This wise woman had lived in the mountains for many years and was known to receive only the poor. She refused to have anything to do with people of wealth or power. Knowing this, the empress disguised herself as a simple peasant and ordered her attendants to wait at the foot of the mountain. She went alone, and when she got up to the dwelling of the old woman, she found her digging in a small garden that obviously fed her. The old wise woman nodded her head in greeting as she continued to work away. The empress said politely, "I've come to ask your help with three questions: What is the best time to do each thing? Who are the most important people to work with? What's the most important thing to do at all times?"

The old wise woman listened but then she only patted the empress on the shoulder and continued digging. Because the empress could see she was an old woman, she said, "You must be tired. Let me give you a hand with that." The empress then picked up another hoe and spade and began to work.

Together they dug a few rows and then the empress stopped and turned to the old woman to ask the three questions again. The wise woman didn't answer. She just kept digging. And finally she said to the empress, "You've helped me. Why don't you take a rest now for a moment? I'll continue." But the empress, too, continued to dig. An hour passed, then two, and the sun got ready to set and the empress grew frustrated. She said, "I've asked you these three questions. If you can't answer them, please let me know. It's getting late and soon I am going to leave."

The old woman said, "Wait, don't you hear someone coming this way? Do you hear that?" The empress turned her head and saw a strange man with a beard emerge from the woods. He was running wildly, pressing his hands into his stomach to cover a big bloody wound. He'd obviously been attacked. He ran until he fell, groaning and half-conscious at the feet of the empress. Opening the man's clothing, the empress saw a deep gash and took off part of her own clothing to stem the bleeding. The wise woman got some medicinal herbs and water and then cleansed the wound before wrapping and binding it in order to help the man heal. Finally, the wounded man regained consciousness and asked for something to drink. The empress ran down to the stream and brought back the fresh cool water. Meanwhile, the sun had disappeared, and it was getting cold. The old wise woman gave the empress a hand in carrying the old man into the hut, where he closed his eyes. Then they all lay down and fell asleep for the night.

When the empress rose the next morning, the sun had already risen. For a moment she forgot why she'd even come to this place. And as she was opening her eyes, the man with the bandaged belly looked over at her and whispered, "Please forgive me. Please forgive me."

"But what have you done that I should forgive you?" the empress said.

"You don't know who I am, your majesty, but I know you," he said. "I was your sworn enemy. I vowed to take vengeance on you because your soldiers killed my brother and took all our property. And when I learned that you were coming alone in the mountains to visit this old woman, I resolved to surprise you on the way back and kill you. But after waiting a long time, there was no sign of you coming down the mountain, so I left my ambush to seek you out and your soldiers saw me. They ran after me, and they took their swords out. I'd intended to kill you, but they stabbed me instead. And when I ran up here, you saved my life. Please forgive me. I'm ashamed of what I was thinking. I am grateful to be your subject, and I will follow you now for I see you as a woman of great compassion. Please grant me your forgiveness."

The empress was overjoyed to see that she had so easily reconciled with a man who'd been her enemy. She not only forgave the man, but she offered to return his property, and she vowed to send her physician to attend to him. And while she was doing this, she noticed that the old woman was outside working in the garden again, as old women do. They know how to plant the earth.

Once again, feeling frustrated, the empress said to the old woman, "I'm happy to be here with you, but you haven't answered my questions. Can you *please* tell me these answers?"

The wise woman looked back and said, "Don't you see, your majesty? Your questions have already been answered."

"How is that?" the empress asked.

"Well, yesterday, if you'd not taken pity on my age and given me a hand with digging these beds, you would've been attacked by this man on the way down. You might have been killed, and you would've deeply regretted not staying with me. Therefore, the most important time was the time you were digging in the beds. And the most important person was me. And the most important pursuit was to be of service, to help. Later, when the wounded man ran up here, the most important time was the time you spent cleaning and dressing his wounds. If you'd not cared for him, he would've died, and you would've lost the chance to be reconciled with him. Likewise, he was the most important person, and the most important pursuit was to be of service and help once more.

"Remember," she went on, "there's only one important time, and that's now. The present moment is the only time over which you have any dominion, over which you have any gift of power. And the most important person is always those you're with, those who are right before you, for who knows what will happen in the future and whether you'll have dealings with anyone else. In this moment, those eyes, that body, that voice, that person is there with you. And the most important pursuit, the one that really tends your heart and makes your life meaningful and worthwhile, is to serve, to bring to that person and to those around you a happiness and a care for that alone is what life is for."

I'M A CLINICAL ASSISTANT at a hospital, and one busy morning at about 8:30 am, an elderly gentleman in his eighties arrived to have stitches removed from his thumb. He said he was in a hurry, as he had an appointment at 9:00 am.

The nurse took his vital signs and had him take a seat, knowing it would be over an hour before someone would be able to see him. I saw him looking at his watch and decided, since I was not busy with another patient, I would evaluate his wound.

Upon exam, I found it well healed, so I talked to one of the doctors and got the needed supplies to remove his sutures and redress his wound. While taking care of his wound, I asked him if he had another doctor's appointment that morning, as he was in such a hurry. The gentleman told me no but that he needed to go to the nursing home to eat breakfast with his wife.

I inquired as to her health. He told me that she had been there for a while and that she was an Alzheimer's disease patient. As we talked, I asked if she would be upset if he was a bit late. He replied that she no longer knew who he was and that she had not recognized him in five years.

I was surprised and asked him, "And you still go every morning, even though she doesn't know who you are?" He smiled as he patted my hand and said, "She doesn't know me, but I still know who she is."

I had to hold back tears as he left. I had goose bumps on my arms as I thought, "That is the kind of love I want in my life."

Do your little bit of good where you are;
it's those little bits of good put together
that overwhelm the world.

DESMOND TUTU

HOW DO WE TRULY OFFER our gifts and our service in the world today? How do we embody a service-oriented way of living in the modern era? We have our tech connections like Snapchat and Instagram and Facebook and email—but they can lack the personal depth and feeling that are required to make service genuine. Chris Whitmore brings this idea alive in the story below:

> During my first year of teaching, a girl named Shay was assigned to my seventh-grade class. She was a desperately unhappy child and rebelled against the most basic rules, such as "Stay in your seat" and "Raise your hand to speak."
>
> Shay and I battled for control of the classroom. I tried every technique I knew: behavior contracts, praise, reprimands. None of them worked. I even called Shay's home every week, but no one answered. (She lived with an older sister.) I went to the school counselor, who said I'd done my duty and offered to transfer Shay to another classroom. I declined. Shay was my student, and I wasn't going to pass her on to someone else. In the faculty lounge the older teachers patted me on the back, thankful they didn't have Shay in their classrooms.
>
> June finally came. On the last day of school, Shay was quick to head out the door. As I sat contemplating my failure with her, she walked back in. Oh, great, I thought: one last act of terrorism.
>
> In Shay's hand was a small bowl, the kind that students made in ceramics class. She thrust it into my grasp. "Here," she said. "It's the only thing I could think of to give you."

I turned the bowl over and saw Shay's initials etched on the bottom.

"Thanks for trying to like me," she said.

Before I could speak, she turned and left.

After several more years of teaching, I went on to become a school principal and am now a district superintendent. Shay's bowl has never left my desk.[2]

MY FRIEND MALIDOMA SOMÉ, a West African medicine man and shaman, said that the Dagara people, his people, teach that every child is born with a special cargo. This is a metaphor drawn from the cargo boats that ply the rivers of West Africa. Malidoma explained that the task of every child and every human being is to deliver their cargo, to bring the gifts that they are born with into the world. If you can't deliver your gifts, then it will be an unfulfilled life for you. To be happy, you have to sense what your cargo is and find your way to offer it to the world. You must trust that it's possible. When you deliver your cargo and act from inner integrity, your good heart serves all.

PLANTING A GARDEN, raising loving children, teaching others, running an ethical business, and offering a smile and a helping hand may seem like small efforts, but together they knit the holy fabric of the world. We can use our gifts in a thousand ways. Celebrated chef José Andrés, who has won many top awards, was inspired to act after a devastating 2010 earthquake in Haiti. He couldn't look aside. He assembled a team and went to Haiti, where he learned to cook the food that most comforted them. They served thousands of meals, and this was the start of the World Central Kitchen (WCK), dedicated to feed people in emergencies when they were most in need. In the years since, thousands of volunteers have joined him. Across earthquake and hurricane disaster areas and amidst the danger in conflicts in Gaza and Ukraine, WCK has served over a hundred million meals across the world. A quote from John Steinbeck's *Grapes of Wrath* can be found on José Andrés's bio page on the WCK website: "Wherever there's a fight so that hungry people may eat, [we'll] be there."

HOW CAN ONE become enlightened?

Love people and feed them.

NEEM KAROLI BABA

I HEARD ABOUT A DOCTOR—we'll call him Dr. Jerry Flaxstead—who described his initial revulsion and difficulty working with to a patient named Frank. Frank was an angry and obese homeless man who had diabetes, was unbathed, and had gangrenous legs and open sores. When he did not take his meds for his mental disorder, Frank would flail his arms and spew epithets and curses at those around him. Frank was admitted repeatedly to the hospital. For Dr. Flaxstead, Frank was a patient who was hard to love.

One day, Frank was brought into the hospital with congestive heart failure. The diagnosis was serious, and Dr. Flaxstead tended him as best as he could. Then twenty members of the down-home neighborhood church, in whose shelter Frank sometimes slept, arrived. They brought flowers and homemade food and chanted and sang hymns to Frank, creating a chorus of care and communion. When Dr. Flaxstead returned to Frank's room after tending to another patient on the ward, he saw that Frank was smiling, bathed in their love. The doctor realized that he had never really seen Frank at all.

TERRY DOBSON HAD GONE to Japan to study martial arts, and on one drowsy spring afternoon, he received a real-life lesson in aikido:

> I was headed to town on a train that clanked and rattled through the suburbs of Tokyo. Our car was comparatively empty—a few housewives with their kids in tow, some old folks going shopping. I gazed absently at the drab houses and dusty hedgerows.
>
> At one station the doors opened, and suddenly the afternoon quiet was shattered by a man bellowing violent, incomprehensible curses as he staggered into our car. He wore laborer's clothing, and he was big, drunk, and dirty. Screaming, he swung at a woman holding a baby. The blow sent her spinning into the laps of an elderly couple. It was a miracle that the baby was unharmed.
>
> Terrified, the couple jumped up and scrambled toward the other end of the car. The laborer aimed a kick at the retreating back of the old woman but missed as she scuttled to safety. This so enraged the drunk that he grabbed the metal pole in the center of the car and tried to wrench it out of its stanchion. I could see that one of his hands was cut and bleeding. The train lurched ahead, the passengers frozen with fear.
>
> I stood up.
>
> I was young then, and in pretty good shape. I'd been putting in a solid eight hours of aikido training nearly every day for the past three years. I like to throw and grapple. I thought I was tough. Trouble was, my martial skill

was untested in actual combat. As students of aikido, we were not allowed to fight.

"Aikido," my teacher had said again and again, "is the art of reconciliation. Whoever has the mind to fight has broken his connection with the universe. If you try to dominate people, you are already defeated. We study how to resolve conflict, not how to start it."

I listened to his words. I tried hard. I even went so far as to cross the street to avoid the chimpira, the pinball punks who lounged around the train stations. My forbearance exalted me. I felt both tough and holy. In my heart, however, I wanted an absolutely legitimate opportunity whereby I might save the innocent by destroying the guilty.

"This is it!" I said to myself, getting to my feet. "People are in danger and if I don't do something fast, they will probably get hurt."

Seeing me stand up, the drunk recognized a chance to focus his rage. "Aha!" He roared. "A foreigner! You need a lesson in Japanese manners!"

I held on lightly to the commuter strap overhead and gave him a slow look of disgust and dismissal. I planned to take this turkey apart, but he had to make the first move. I wanted him mad, so I pursed my lips and blew him an insolent kiss.

"All right!" He hollered. "You're gonna get a lesson." He gathered himself for a rush at me.

A split second before he could move, someone shouted, "HEY!"

It was earsplitting. I remember the strangely joyous, lilting quality of it—as though you and a friend had been searching diligently for something, and he suddenly stumbled upon it.

"HEY!"

I wheeled to my left; the drunk spun to his right. We both stared down at a little old Japanese man. He must have been well into his seventies, this tiny gentleman, sitting there immaculate in his kimono. He took no notice of me, but beamed delightedly at the laborer, as though he had a most important, most welcome secret to share.

"C'mere," the old man said in an easy vernacular, beckoning to the drunk. "C'mere and talk with me." He waved his hand lightly.

The big man followed, as if on a string. He planted his feet belligerently in front of the old gentleman, and roared above the clacking wheels, "Why the hell should I talk to you?"

The drunk now had his back to me. If his elbow moved so much as a millimeter, I'd drop him in his socks.

The old man continued to beam at the laborer.

"What'cha been drinkin'?" he asked, his eyes sparkling with interest.

"I been drinkin' sake," the laborer bellowed back, "and it's none of your business!"

Flecks of spittle spattered the old man.

"Oh, that's wonderful," the old man said, "absolutely wonderful! You see, I love sake, too. Every night, me and my wife (she's 76, you know), we warm up a little bottle of sake and take it out into the garden, and we sit on an old wooden bench. We watch the sun go down, and we look to see how our persimmon tree is doing. My great-grandfather planted that tree, and we worry about whether it will recover from those ice storms we had last winter. Our tree has done better than I expected, especially when you consider the poor quality of the soil. It is gratifying to watch when we take our sake and go out to enjoy the evening—even when it rains!"

He looked up at the laborer, eyes twinkling.

As he struggled to follow the old man's conversation, the drunk's face began to soften. His fists slowly unclenched.

"Yeah," he said. "I love persimmons too . . ." His voice trailed off.

"Yes," said the old man, smiling, "and I'm sure you have a wonderful wife."

"No," replied the laborer. "My wife died."

Very gently, swaying with the motion of the train, the big man began to sob.

"I don't got no wife, I don't got no home, I don't got no job. I am so ashamed of myself."

Tears rolled down his cheeks; a spasm of despair rippled through his body.

Now it was my turn. Standing there in my well-scrubbed, youthful innocence and make-this-world-safe-for-democracy righteousness, I suddenly felt dirtier than he was.

Then the train arrived at my stop. As the doors opened, I heard the old man cluck sympathetically.

"My, my," he said, "that is a difficult predicament, indeed. Sit down here and tell me about it."

I turned my head for one last look. The laborer was sprawled on the seat, his head in the old man's lap. The old man was softly stroking the filthy, matted hair.

As the train pulled away, I sat down on a bench. What I had wanted to do with muscle had been accomplished with kind words. I had just seen aikido tried in combat, and the essence of it was love. I would have to practice the art with an entirely different spirit. It would be a long time before I could speak about the resolution of combat.[3]

JANET LUTZ, A HOSPITAL CHAPLAIN, tells of how she goes around her hospital and blesses the people who work there. She said it's not a practice she invented:

> One of the things we do is, we go around and bless the hands of all the people who work in the hospital. Of course I bless the nurses and doctors. But I especially want to go around to find the people in the basement and the people who are cleaning the toilets and people who are serving the food. And when I go around finding people, wherever they are, they're often startled, and then really touched by it, as am I. . . . You know, these people work really hard and are so essential, but often not seen by patients and families.[4]

Give me everything mangled and bruised,
And I will make a light of it to make you weep.
And we will have rain,
And begin again.

DEENA METZGER

IN ANCIENT GREECE, the Furies—vengeance, anger, and jealousy—appear when truth is not being honored, when oaths are not being kept, and when the honorable respect that people have pledged their life to has been undermined and betrayed. They appear even now in our modern times. And when the Furies are released, nothing can stop them—not prayers or even the intervention of the gods.

When the truth was not honored in ancient Greece, and the Furies' destruction arose, the goddess of wisdom, Athena, understood what was needed. She did not condemn them or fear them. Instead, she invited the Furies into her temple of wisdom, made a place for them there, and said, "You too must have a place here. Even you, anger and jealousy. All of you can come in." She made an altar for them as if to say, "Even the Furies that arise in us out of deep betrayal and vengeance can be held in the temple of wisdom. Then the world will come together again."

THE COLOMBIAN CIVIL WAR was a violent conflict that lasted over fifty years. It seemed almost impossible to find a resolution. One month, in the later stages of peace negotiation, the government tried something different: They filled helicopters with photographs and went to the areas of the jungle where the Revolutionary Armed Forces of Colombia, a guerrilla group of revolutionaries also known as the People's Army, had been living for decades. There, they dropped photographs of their families out of the helicopter doors, pictures of their old mothers and fathers, their sisters and brothers, and the grown-up nieces and nephews they'd never seen. They dropped these photos right down into the places the army was residing. Each photograph was marked on the back with the names of the people in the photos, so that the people who'd been away as fighters for ten or fifteen or twenty years knew who each photo belonged to. Their hope was that when they saw the photos of their family members, they would remember that they were connected to something bigger. They were reminded that they had someone, something, to love. It was a critical step in helping the revolutionaries lay down their arms. The connection to love helped turn the conflict around.

HOW DO YOU HOLD the conflicts in your life? Here are the Buddha's instructions:

> Look how he abused me and beat me,
> How he threw me down and robbed me.
> Live with such thoughts and you live in hate.
> Look how he abused me and beat me,
> How he threw me down and robbed me.
> Abandon such thoughts, and live in love.
> Hatred never ends by hatred,
> but by love alone it is healed.
> This is the ancient and eternal law.[5]

Yes, many bad and painful things happen to us and to the world. We need to see them clearly and protect others and ourselves. We must do so with courage. And also with unwavering compassion. And always remember: Hatred will never dispel hatred. In the end, it is love that transforms it all.

We can make our minds so like still water that beings gather about us that they may see their own images, and so live for a moment with a clearer, perhaps even a fiercer life because of our quiet.

WILLIAM BUTLER YEATS

It was a new old man behind the counter,
skinny, brown, and eager.
He greeted me like a long-lost daughter,
as if we both came from the same world,
someplace warmer and more gracious than this
    cold city.

I was thirsty, and alone. Sick at heart, grief-soiled,
    and his face lit up as if I were his prodigal daughter

returning,
coming back to the freezer bins in front of the register
which were still and always filled
with the same old Cable Car ice-cream sandwiches
    and cheap frozen greens.
Back to the knobs of beef and packages of hot dogs,
these familiar shelves strung with potato chips
    and corn chips,
stacked-up beer boxes and immortal Jim Beam.

I lumbered to the case and bought my precious
    bottled water
and he returned my change, beaming
as if I were the bright new buds on the just-
    bursting-open cherry trees,
as if I were everything beautiful struggling to grow,
and he was blessing me as he handed me my dime

over the dirty counter and the plastic tub of red
    licorice whips.
This old man who didn't speak English
beamed out love to me in the iron week after my
    mother's death
so that when I emerged from his store

    my whole cockeyed life—
    what a beautiful failure!—
glowed gold like a sunset after rain.

    Frustrated city dogs were yelping in their yards,
mad with passion behind their chain-link fences,
    and in the driveway of a peeling-paint house
    a woman and a girl danced to contagious reggae.

Praise Allah! Jah! The Buddha! Kwan Yin,
Jesus, Mary, and even jealous old Jehovah!

For eyes, hands
of the divine, everywhere.

            ALISON LUTERMAN[6]

MINDFULNESS IS NOT PASSIVE. It isn't about having your eyes closed. It isn't just about presence. First there is mindful presence and then there is mindful response. In Zen, it is taught this way:

> There are only two things:
> You sit and you sweep the garden.
> It doesn't matter how big the garden is.
>
> You sit and then you get up
> and sweep the garden of the world.

MR. ROGERS DESCRIBES how his mother taught him to see the disasters of the world in a new way. Instead of focusing just on the tragedy and loss, she said, look for the helpers. Expand your gaze to take in all the people who are rushing in from all sides to offer their care and assistance and support. Amidst the hard times let yourself see the wave of compassion that arises around the suffering. The human heart that cannot be stopped.

IN 2017, A GROUP OF VOLUNTEERS with bass boats, airboats, and other recreational vessels—part of what they called the Cajun Navy—set off in caravans from Baton Rouge, Louisiana, all bound for hurricane- and flood-devastated Houston.

A nine-hour drive delivered this impromptu flotilla to a sheriff's training facility, where the volunteers stayed for the night. The next day, the group launched its vessels in Humble, Texas, about twenty miles north of Houston, navigating by the interstate that had become an uncharted river.

With little formal organization, the Cajun Navy has gradually expanded. Boats come from Mississippi and Alabama and Arkansas. They have come to the rescue in many disasters, such as Hurricane Katrina in 2005, and have continued to come to the aid of emergency workers during catastrophic floods in the south ever since.

"We're trying to do what we can," said Ben Theriot, an engineer whose house near Baton Rouge was flooded in the storms. "I had people that I barely knew showing up to help me. The best way you can thank somebody for helping you is to go help somebody else."[7]

After plucking stranded residents from an apartment complex and people and animals from rooftops, the men, tired and soaking wet, hauled their boats out and hit the road, responding to reports of more flooding on the Texas coast.

The Cajun Navy now reappears in response to floods whenever it is needed. They launch their small boats to become a mighty armada whenever flooding and disaster call.

Live in joy, in love, even among those who hate.
Live in joy, in health, even among the afflicted.
Live in joy, in peace, even among the troubled.
Look within, be still.
Free from fear and attachment,
Know the sweet joy of living in the Way.

THE BUDDHA

IN THE FORESTS of the wilder parts of the borders of Laos and Thailand and Cambodia, there has been enormous loss. The burning and cutting down of the trees have been happening for decades. When my teachers were first living in these forests and jungles, there were tigers and elephants and wild bulls. Then modernization changed it all. Forests were cut down, and the natural world was decimated, affecting all the animals. And so the forest monks decided on a compassionate response. Some of the abbots and the monastics went out into the remaining stands of forest, took off their robes, and put them on the great old teak trees. They ordained the trees as abbots of the forest and went through all the chanting and rituals to make it so. And because there was such reverence and belief in the sacredness of the robes and the monastics, that part of the forest has remained untouched.

Your mind is like a piece of land planted with many different kinds of seeds: seeds of joy, peace, mindfulness, understanding, and love; seeds of craving, anger, fear, hate, and forgetfulness. These wholesome and unwholesome seeds are always there, sleeping in the soil of your mind. The quality of your life depends on the seeds you water. If you plant tomato seeds in your gardens, tomatoes will grow. Just so, if you water a seed of peace in your mind, peace will grow. When the seeds of happiness in you are watered, you will become happy. When the seed of anger in you is watered, you will become angry. The seeds that are watered frequently are those that will grow strong.

THICH NHAT HANH

THE STORY THAT FOLLOWS, in its original form, was written by Jean Giono, a celebrated French author who became a pacifist after seeing the horrors of the World Wars. When I witnessed the monks of the Thai forest tradition wrap their robes around trees, I felt inspired to rewrite Jean's story and set it in Asia. In the 1980s I called Madame Giono, the late author's wife, and she graciously gave me permission to share this new version. It reminds us that we can all make a difference.

❂

My name is Lin Shan, and I have become a Taoist monk in the Chinese Mountain Spring lineage. I learned about the Natural Way from Li Pung, who is now an old man with a thin grey beard who sweeps the path to a Taoist temple outside the prosperous village of Feng Shr Li.

The village where he lives was not always so prosperous. Indeed it stood on barren land with only a few of the most rudimentary huts for the three or four families who eked out a living grazing a few scrawny animals and planting seeds in the dry, bony soil with a prayer for their growth. Most often their prayers were not answered.

This desolation is not new to China. Oh, it is a sad story and an old one. You who have a chance to know what is befalling the last forests of our modern times should consider it well, for China has not always been bereft of forests. Forests hold the soul of the land and the greenness of their trees breathes life back into the air that we breathe together. The fluttering of their leaves like the white barked Chinese aspen has given rise to our greatest

Chinese poetry. A thousand years ago, Li Po walked through such magical forests and meditated there until his heart was clear and his thoughts flew away like clouds before the wind. He wrote,

> We sat together, the forest and I
> Merging into silence
> Until only the forest remained.

Those among us fortunate enough to have entered a great and beautiful forest even once in our life cannot forget such a memory, the spring in our feet, the vibrancy of our breath, and the joy of the cells of our body.

But now the forests of China are dead. They have been dead for five hundred years or a thousand years or two thousand years. There are so many of us. We have cut them down to build homes, for cooking and for warmth, to clear the land for yet one more field. And our land has become barren. The soil has run into our rivers. The ancient and winding yellow river was not always so, but for centuries now it has flowed yellow like our tears with soil eroding year after year from our barren lands.

Even young children know something is wrong, never seeing a great forest or hearing the cries of birds in its treetops and stopping for the noises of unseen animals. These children know something is missing. They hear ancient stories of the wolves and bear that lived in the forests, the stories of wild pig and Chinese mountain tigers. Their hearts, too, must long for a time when the forests were alive and when human life was more fully alive.

But all is not lost. The village of Feng Shr Li sits at the foot of the Feng Shr valley, which is again filled with glades of bamboo and running streams. Beyond them a whole range of low hills and mountains in the distance is covered by the sweet scent of Chinese forest. One day, my friend Li Pung sat down from his sweeping and told me how this forest returned.

At the end of the last century, there lived in this valley a man who the Taoists now revere as a dragon (which for the Taoists means the Spirit come alive on earth). Li Pung tells me his name was Tam Yang Bun, and he was born in a desolate village half a province from here near the Lo Chu riverbed. Now they say that as he grew up he loved to visit the old Taoist temple along the dry riverbank of the Lo Chu. But he was a dutiful son as we are taught to be (those were still the days of the Confucian system that lasted for more than two thousand years). As a dutiful son, he worked the land for his parents and being gifted with a mind of brightness began to write poetry and read at a young age. Sensing his potential, his parents hired a tutor to visit as was the custom in those days, to prepare for the Confucian examinations. Taking the lowest level at age twelve, he showed promise and the county itself supported his further studies. He passed successfully the medium and higher level examinations. Had he been born of a good family he might even have gone to the capitol to stand for the examinations known as the Emperor's Blessings. But he was not and so was prepared to work for the local magistrate.

A marriage was arranged to a lovely woman from several villages away. Pigs were offered as is our local custom, an appropriate wedding ensued, and for one year they lived happily and were graced by a child.

Then the sorrows came. First his young child, Most Precious Gift, died of pneumonia, and his father, though not old, died in the influenza epidemic that same year. His wife, stricken with grief, became thin and pale, and she too died within a year. His old mother sought refuge in a small Taoist nunnery at the foot of the Tai Shung mountains, and he was left with his heart as desolate as the lands around him. He could not return to his old home village. He left the magistrate, taking a few clothes and several volumes of Taoist poetry and disappearing up into the mountains.

Li Pung says he first met Tam Yang Bun when, as a young man, he went off walking and hunting in those desolate mountains beyond the Taoist temple that is now his home. He had walked far into the mountains after hearing at a farm house of a strange Taoist priest who was seen occasionally living far beyond the settlement. As he walked far into the Feng Shr valley, he came upon an amazing sight—one whole part of the hillside was filled with young and beautifully growing Chinese shen trees, their delicate leaves fluttering in the breeze. He couldn't understand how this young and beautiful forest had begun so far up in the hills. He sat down with a certain joy among the saplings and saw a Chinese ground squirrel run behind the rocks nearby. From where the forest had begun to grow, the animals who came with it had begun to take shelter.

In the distance he heard a *ching ching* and then nothing, and then a *ching ching* again and then nothing. Rousing himself, he walked toward the sound and that is when he first met Tam Yang Bun.

Though thin and simply clad, Tam Yang Bun gave off an air that was neither blank nor impoverished. There was a grace and economy in his movements and a stillness about him that belied his strength. His skin was dark from the sun, and his eyes were bright and steady. He could have been any age from thirty-five to seventy-five, but this is often the case with those Taoist priests who have studied the immortal arts. Tam Yang Bun looked at Li Pung steadily for a minute or two while he approached and then returned to his work. He was carrying a curved wooden staff, a Taoist divining rod with a long brass point at its lower end. He would walk several paces along the hillside and then *ching ching*, the staff opened a hole in the earth at a small level spot or place where the earth seemed receptive. Into this he dropped one or two of the small shen tree pods, gently covering the hole with a sweep of his foot, moving several paces away to *ching ching* in another spot. It was steady peaceful work, and you could see that Tam Yang Bun had already planted a series of long rows along this hillside.

Li Pung sat and watched him for nearly an hour when finally he stopped and sat on a rock outcropping to rest. Li Pung brought his satchel of food to share, glutinous rice balls and vegetable paste, and offered them to Tam Yang Bun. They shared the lunch in peaceful silence. Finally Li Pung asked if he might stay with Tam Yang Bun for the afternoon. Tam Yang Bun replied simply by handing him a sack of shen tree pods with a great smile. Li Pung asked several more questions and, as an answer each time, received more silence than words. When Li Pung asked if Tam Yang Bun had planted the entire young and beautiful forest in these hills and how long it had taken, Tam Yang Bun finally laughed and said, "The earth replenished herself with the help of the Tao."

This was to be the first of many encounters with Tam Yang Bun, but Li Pung did not know it at the time. He knew nothing of Tam Yan Bun's life, which would be revealed to him many years later. He only knew that he felt a peace and steadiness in this man's presence, steady like warm sunlight and receptive like mountain-stream water entering dry earth. He sensed there was some simple power working here through the shen pods and the land and the *ching ching* of the wood and brass pole, and he knew it was part of the Tao he had sought.

Li Pung visited several times in the next few years. Once on a cold winter day, he came upon Tam Yang Bun standing like an enormous bird in the crane posture wearing only a modest bathing cloth. In the cold air, his deep and directed breathing sent a pulsating cloud in front of him. As Li Pung got closer he could see the shining of Tam Yang Bun's eyes and a remarkable glow upon his skin.

Tam Yang Bun taught him some of the secrets of caring for the forest. He showed him how to soak the shen tree pods in a spring for two days to soften them for planting and rapid growth. He created a small orchard and an upland nursery for hundreds of new saplings. Always when Li Pung returned, the forest was growing, and new hillsides were covered with saplings. The streams seemed fuller, and the young forest rustled with wildlife as if the animals had felt the hospitality return again to the land. Mouse deer were sighted, and other animals from the high mountains began to return to the hills around the Feng Shr valley. Li Pung felt in this forest as if he were entering a graceful and ancient Chinese scroll, the watercolors of mountains and wilderness painted by the masters of old.

Li Pung, still a young man, then moved to one of the eight central provinces to continue his studies of The Analects and the philosophies of the middle kingdom. Even as he studied, the last of the Confucian examinations were being held and from a distance came news of the Boxer Rebellion. There were rumors of gunshots and of wars over tea and opium as some great new forces swept over the land of China.

Soon the new nation was in chaos, the armies of warlords were fighting from many sides and many factions. Revolution completed its process and Sun Yat-sen was made president. It was during this period that Li Pung was to be married. He played a small role in the revolution and spent a short time in the revolutionary student movement but long enough to know he did not have to follow the ways of his parents, nor take the bride assigned to him by traditional village custom. He recognized that what his parents wanted of him did not fit his true nature.

With such upheaval in China, Li Pung longed to return to his home. He did so and found his village much unchanged but strangely more prosperous. The streams that had been small or nonexistent had more water coursing through them. There were new dikes, and water was led across newly planted fields, somehow more fertile than he remembered. The land was softer, more alive, and less desolate. Up in the hills, Tam Yang Bun continued his work as if the great rebellion had not happened. He continued his planting of several large hillsides, of a whole mountainside, then moved on to other land further back in the valley. He had added Chinese alder, whose tender bark makes fine food for the increasing number of small deer and other animals, to the forests. It was not many days before Li Pung climbed from these mountains to look for his friend. The shade and moisture of the trees had somehow grown and brought with them their sisters, the clouds, and rivulets of water moved in the ground where the forest had matured, a moisture that brought the entire land alive again. As usual, Tam Yang Bun said little to Li Pung but shared most generously his balance and timeless spirit. The forest was growing by hundreds of rai in several directions and, on some days, Tam Yang Bun took Li Pung on long walks to care for the areas of new growth.

Descending to his village, Li Pung felt drawn to the Taoist temple. Leaving the world of examinations and revolutions behind, he formally entered the temple and commenced his study of the Way. Over the first several years, the handful of monks there completed his training in the eight forms and began to demonstrate the unlearning which marks the art of the Tao. He heard the stories of Lao-tzu and Chuang-tzu and saw them brought alive by the monks in the Taoist kitchen and garden, in their mixing of herbs and in their economy of movement. He learned the Taoist postures and energy circulation meditation.

Li Pung studied under the two oldest teachers of the temple and gradually made it his home. When Li Pung's mother died, he performed the ceremony to honor his ancestors and then committed his days to the Taoist order. For twenty-one years Li Pung lived in that temple. He would occasionally walk up into the mountains to visit Tam Yang Bun when he could find him. Some were now calling Tam Yang Bun by a new name: Mountain Tao. Others called him a tree spirit. The forests continued to grow.

When the next wave of revolution swept China with the Japanese invasion, there came the death of the emperor himself. China was again in great disarray and Li Pung stayed cloistered in the temple for those years, wrapping himself in the practices of the Tao. When an interlude of peace descended on the land, Li Pung walked into Feng Shr valley to look for Tam Yang Bun. He was amazed at how beautifully the forest had developed, how dense the trees had become and how Chinese maple, red crested woodpeckers, civet cats, and even tracks of wild boar could be seen among the trees. He was also astonished to see the beginnings of several new villages below the valley. The land was no longer desolate, and the streams flowed clear and fresh. Li Pung climbed into the mountains. He saw a poem written on a rock as he climbed, a favorite of the ancient master, Cold Mountain:

> When people see me,
> They all say, "he's a bit crazy,"
> Not much to look at,
> Dressed in rags and hides.
> Seated among the clouds,
> Wandering like the moon on water,
> All I can say to those I meet,
> "try and make it to Cold Mountain."

Li Pung knew he was on the right trail.

Remarkably, Tam Yang Bun was planting the day he arrived. He could tell by the *ching ching* in the distance. When he encountered his old friend, they embraced and Li Pung knew it was time to come and live with his master. He stayed with Tam Yang Bun for seven years and was taught to eat the herbs of the forest and perform the Taoist exercises of drawing the cream of heaven down through the limbs of the body. Every third moon they performed a ceremony to make the oldest trees honorary monks of the Taoist temple. And in his years in the mountains, Li Pung learned the story of Tam Yang Bun's early sorrows and his mastery of the Tao. He learned from Tam Yang Bun's own teachers—the wind, the rocks, and the trees. He learned a harmony so deep it could not be called by any name. The two men lived together in the Tao and *ching ching* became their music. They lived as the Tao taught:

>The spirit of the valley never dies, it is called the
>>Subtle and the profoundly receptive.
>
>To hold and fill to overflowing is not as good as to
>>Stop in time.
>
>The best of humans is like water. Water is good, it
>>Benefits all things and does not compete with
>>Them. The wise man places himself in the
>>Background and finds himself in the foreground.
>
>He lets go and the spirit moves through him.

Then Li Pung fell ill and could not remain in the mountains. Even the Tao has its seasons and difficulties. He returned to the monastery. Now over ten thousand rai had been reclaimed and planted. The new villages were prospering, small dikes and paddies shone in the morning sun. Goats and pigs squealed under the houses, and there was the laughter of children as new families thrived on this once desolate land. The villages had built new schools, and the children were already accustomed to white rice from the paddy, forgetting the days when glutinous mountain rice was all that would grow. There was a singing like springtime from the streams.

I, Lin Shan, who have been telling you this story, was born at the end of Mao's great triumph. It is a sad triumph for me because few are left of our five million monks of the Taoist and Buddhist way. But a few old men like Master Li Pung were allowed to remain in the temples and somehow as a young boy, I, too, was called there. My heart went to join him and learn the way of the Tao. So I have lived with him these past eight years and heard the stories and practiced the eight measures. Several times I have climbed into the forest to look for Tam Yang Bun, but there has been no sign of him. I thought perhaps he had died but then one day in the far distance, I heard the *ching ching* sound of the immortal Mountain Way. And now I have decided to go to the mountains. It is also my Way. I write this story for you as I leave. Li Pung has taught me the secret of soaking shen tree pods and shown me the fire herbs that bring the body warmth in winter. Sometimes I feel there is not much honor left for the Tao in our temples, and I am called to these mountains, to the animals that roam there, to the sweetness of the forest valleys.

I know there is desolation where you live also. I know that your forests have been lost and that many of your friends do not know who they are. But the earth will not always be desolate, and the Tao has its cycle of return. Perhaps one of you who reads this story will know the spirit of immortality in your heart and go off to the mountains to replant the forests of this earth.[8]

AT NINETY YEARS OLD, poet Gary Snyder, one of America's greatest environmentalists and a visionary of bioregionalism, was interviewed by my friend and colleague Wes Nisker. Gary, who won the Pulitzer Prize, has been writing about the environment for more than fifty years. He is also a celebrated Zen teacher. Wes asked Gary about how we should deal with the increasing intensification of the climate crisis, global warming, the rising oceans, and the loss of species. Gary paused, quietly looked back at Wes, and said, "Don't feel guilty! Guilt and anger and fear are part of the problem. If you want to save the world, save it because you love it."

Guilt, anger, grasping, and fear are the very forces that are causing the difficulty. If you're going to save it, save it as an act of love, not as an act of war. Save it because you love it.

Because love is the only power that has the force to match the suffering that is happening. Love is the force that allows mothers to lift entire cars off their children when there has been an accident. When you are powered by the force of love, it's not a sacrifice to care. It is what you do.

IN THE JATAKA TALES, the Buddha described many of his past lives and in them all he was dedicated to compassion. You could say that in all those lives he was practicing to become a Buddha.

In one of those lives he was born as a friendly little parrot in a great forest. He lived happily and delightedly there. He loved flying through the branches. He made friends with many other creatures. And his spirit was one of joy and happiness in caring for others.

One day, the skies over the forest turned dark, and a huge storm with lightning and thunder filled the air. When the storm ended its flashing and roaring, the wind began to howl. And in the day that followed, the atmosphere became turbulent, and lightning struck and crackled again. One of the trees was struck by lightning, and in its core there was planted a seed of fire. As the forest dried out, that seed sparked a huge fire. Smoke began to rise and flames soon spread, and the animals, terrified, ran wildly in every direction, seeking safety.

When the little parrot smelled the smoke, he flung himself out bravely into the fury of the fire, crying out, "Fire, fire! You must run!" Many of the animals ran to the safety of the river, but others were trapped by the flames and the smoke and couldn't do so. Rather than flying to safety himself, the parrot continued circling over the raging fire, seeking some means to help all those he knew were on the forest floor. And suddenly, a desperate idea came to him. He darted down to the river. He soaked his bird body in the water and then flew back into the raging inferno as if he was unconcerned about the flames. He dropped down low to find anyone he knew from the forest. And when he found his friends, a squirrel or a badger or any animal at all, he would shake the water from the river that was on his body to give the other animal some moments of cooling. The water on his parrot back became like little jewels of life.

Again and again, he flew back to the river, got himself wet, looked for someone who was in danger, some creature, and dripped as many drops of water as he could upon them. His lungs ached. He was dizzy from the flames, but he thought, *What else can I do but fly? I must do this to help.* (Remember, this is the Buddha as the parrot.)

It just so happens that up in heaven, some of the gods and goddesses, resting in their gorgeous palaces, looked down and saw the forest fire, and they saw that something interesting was happening. They said, "Look at that little parrot, how completely foolish he is trying to put out a raging forest fire with his own little wings! Whoever heard of such a thing? It's absurd!" But one of the gods looked closer and found himself somehow strangely moved by the parrot going into the river, coming out, and shaking the water on others. He was so moved that he turned himself into a golden eagle and flew down from heaven to visit and have a closer look. The little parrot was nearing the flames again when the eagle with molten gold wings appeared at his side and said, "Go back, little bird. This is a forest fire. You can't stop this. What can a few drops of water do?"

But the little parrot wouldn't listen. He continued to fly doggedly into the river and back into the flames.

"Save yourself," said the great eagle. And little parrot said, "I don't need a great shining eagle to give me advice, thank you. My mother could have told me that. I just need someone to help." Seeing the parrot flying so steadily through the searing flames again, the eagle thought with shame about his own privileged life. He could see the carefree gods looking down on the earth as if life was just a game. He could hear their laughter, but he also could hear the cries of the creatures in the forest. He wanted to be brave like the parrot. He began to weep streams of tears. And when the gods weep, it turns into rain. As the eagle cried, the clouds opened in the skies and rain poured down, cooling the fire, easing the entire forest with a deluge of the shimmering tears of the gods.

When the flames died down and the smoke began to clear, the little parrot, washed and bright, rocketed in the sky above and laughed. "Now that's more like it!" he said. "Thank you, great eagle!"

Tears dripped from all the burned branches and scorched buds, and the water reminded them that they could flower again. All the animals looked at one another in amazement, and in the blue sky they saw the little parrot doing loop the loops as the forest fire was put out.

※

The power that will motivate us to help the world is our tears. We must let ourselves feel, just as the golden eagle did so bravely. We have to allow ourselves to be touched. It's not enough to be a bystander. The tears you shed will become the tears of your loving care.

WHEN YOU WALK into Ajahn Chah's monastery, you enter a place of peace. There is a kind of impeccable care and dignified discipline about the monks. And their inner beauty is mirrored by the outer beauty made visible through the way they care for the forest and the paths and even their robes.

Little signs, simple and graceful, hang on the walks as you enter. "Be quiet. We're trying to meditate. This is not the city." And "Life is short. What matters to you?" These tiny Dharma signs serve as gentle but big reminders.

Ajahn Chah's forest monastery became a place that reminded all who came of another way to be. It was situated in a province near the border of Cambodia and Laos. During the time of the Indochina Wars involving America, Vietnam, Laos, and Cambodia, we could see flyovers of jets and bombers from the US airbase nearby.

I had worked on Thai tropical medicine teams in the Peace Corps, and some friends from the similar International Voluntary Services in Vietnam and Laos came to visit. When they arrived, they had compelling questions: "What are you doing sitting on your butt when there's a war going on, where unthinkable and cruel things are happening and suffering is enormous? Why don't you come back out and continue to help in some way?" They came from the struggle of the war and stayed in the monastery for about a week.

As the days passed, they began to unnwind and realized the power of the monastery as a zone of peace. They talked to Ajahn Chah about it, and he said, "For those of us who live as monks in this thousand-year-old tradition, wars come and go. Our task is to create a place of sanity that reminds people of the possibility of a steady heart even when there's great difficulty. People forget that there is another way. People need to know what it looks like to take good care of one another." And it was true: In the war zone, you had to be careful because your life was in danger. Everything you had could be stolen. But in the monastery, if you did something as simple as drop an earring, someone would pick it up and place it on the altar until you came back. It was a place of integrity and tremendous care. A true island of sanity.

Ajahn Chah said, "We human beings are constantly at war. We try to fight against and escape anything we think we can't control. And we continue to create suffering, wage war with evil, wage war with good, wage war with what is too small, wage war with what is too big, with what is too short or too long, right or wrong. We carry on the battle. Why not stop the war? Why not step out of the battle and come to a place of peace?"

It isn't that we just have to do away with landmines and bombings on the planet. We also have to do away with the landmines in the human heart. We have to do away with the violence in the human heart. We see modern society still caught in racism and environmental destruction and continuing warfare. Where does it come from? It comes from us. We have to come to a place of compassion in order to find a different way.

As Ajahn Chah says, let your heart and mind become still no matter what your surroundings. Find the quiet place within you and let your mind become like a clear forest pool. Then you will know how to live.

Do not ignore the effect of each wise
action saying, "This will come to nothing."
Just as by the gradual fall of raindrops
the water jar is filled, so in time the
wise become replete with good.

DHAMMAPADA

MANY WESTERNERS came to learn from Ajahn Chah. Because most of them did not speak Thai he said, "Why don't we make a monastery where the teachings are in English?" So in a forest nearby, villagers built a beautiful monastery where thirty or more Westerners were able to live. And one American woman, who came to be a nun, was an exemplar of dedication. She learned the language and became one of the villagers' favorites. But after about five years, she left without much notice. People were disappointed. They respected her and enjoyed listening to her newly found Buddhist wisdom. And they missed her good spirit.

After a year had passed, she came back to visit. While she was away, she had met a great evangelist and became a born-again Christian. When she returned to the monastery, she tried to tell everybody that the true way to practice was through Jesus.

Naturally this evangelism upset the Western monks and nuns and even more it upset the local villagers who had loved supporting her. They had built a Buddhist monastery, and now the most charismatic of the nuns was trying to make them Christian.

So a group of villagers and monks walked the ten miles over the rice fields to Ajahn Chah's main monastery. They recounted how she had come back and was trying to convert everybody. Ajahn Chah listened to them all. He knew this was happening. The grapevine between monasteries is like any other grapevine. "How could she do this?" they said. "We fed her and trusted her, and now she's come back and betrayed us!"

After listening for a very long time, Ajahn Chah got very quiet. They all wondered what he would say.

He smiled as he said, "Well, maybe she's right."

They all laughed. He wasn't attached. Everybody started out on their high horse about how it was supposed to be. Now they returned to their village smiling and not taking it all so seriously.

This wisdom might help in some of the conflicts we face today. Maybe there's something that needs to be listened to from someone who is different. It doesn't mean you can't respond when there is harm and injustice. There are many things that we need to stand up for. But as Ajahn Chah taught, we must be discerning. Sometimes fighting against someone's views is unnecessary. And sometimes, we are fighting against something that isn't causing any harm. Not really. We can stop adding to the war.

He who would do good to another,
must do it in Minute Particulars.

WILLIAM BLAKE

THE EARTH WANTS to renew itself. You give it a little bit of water, a few seeds planted here and there, and then all of a sudden something happens. The earth knows it's alive. It is part of us. And it speaks to us.

When the government tried to suppress the truth of the Chernobyl nuclear disaster, the wind told the story. The wind carried the truth across nations. The wind was a poet, a scientist, and a prophet. The earth wants to work with us to renew it itself, and we get to plant the seeds. Wangari Maathai, who won the Nobel Prize for the greenbelts in East Africa, planted fifty-one million trees. She and her friends did that one tree at a time. Things can change. And we have the opportunity to make that change happen by working with the earth. One tree at a time. There is so much hope in steadily planting seeds, raising our voices, adding our care every day.

THE PRACTICE OF mindful loving awareness and compassion empowers us to reflect and choose what we will do. Some acts will be political, some will be to plant trees, some will be to support justice, and some will be to educate. All are good.

When you feel empowered to make a difference, it will not only change the earth as you plant those seeds, but it will also change your heart. You don't want to die feeling like you didn't do anything. If you contribute, not out of anger, not out of fear, not out of hatred or aggression, but out of love, you will be happy.

Molly Ivins, a humorist, celebrated journalist, and courageous activist, advised, "Keep fighting for freedom and justice, beloveds, but don't forget to have fun doin' it. Be outrageous... rejoice in all the oddities that freedom can produce. And when you get through celebrating the sheer joy of a good fight, be sure to tell those who come after how much fun it was!"[9]

HERE THE UNITED NATIONS Climate Summit speaks to us:

One day we will wake up to find that the energy that powers the alarm clock came from the breeze through the trees the night before. And we will go to work that morning riding the rays of the sun. It will light our cities and power our businesses; it will warm our homes and cool our workplaces; it will reduce sources of conflict and fuel our economies. It will connect us all. It won't scar the land or poison the seas. The food we eat will be good for our bodies and good for the planet, and the weather that day won't make us worry for tomorrow. There will be more jobs and less disease. The sea level will stop rising and species will stop dying. The question is how do we get to that day from where we are today?

All 8 billion of us.

We start by deciding that beyond our doubts and differences such a day truly exists; and that is something each of us can do today. We can make today the day we stop thinking that the changes to get there are impossible and beyond us, and start realizing that they are not only possible, but what the future requires of us. We must stop turning from the warnings from science that bring fear and denial, and instead turn toward the solutions and partnerships we need. We can make today the day we stop pointing at each other in blame and instead chart a new course together. We have never faced a crisis this big, but we have never had a better opportunity to solve it. We have everything we need to wake up to a different kind of world. We need our leaders to be brave and their choices to be bold. They will either remember us as the generation that destroyed its home or the one that finally came to respect it. We have every reason in the world to act. We can't wait until tomorrow.

This is your only home; you can choose today to make a world of difference.[10]

PRACTICE

Living with Climate Change

Climate change has become one of the most important questions of our time. How do we each live with it? How do we practice with it? Do we respond out of fear, heartbreak, despair, denial, or anger? One map that may be helpful is the four noble truths of the Buddhist teachings.

The first of these noble truths is the noble truth of suffering. It doesn't say life is suffering. It says life *has* suffering, and to find freedom you need to acknowledge this reality. You can't pretend you don't have it. It doesn't matter how successful you are; you're going to have it. There's joy and sorrow, gain and loss, pleasure and pain. You're going to have hurts and aging and conflict and difficulty.

You can also say this is the first noble truth of climate change itself. The level of CO_2 in the atmosphere is now higher than it's been in three million years. Every year we're burning more carbon, and we're only beginning to feel the impact of that change in the atmosphere. The blanket of CO_2 is joined by enormous releases of methane gas, which is impacting the environment more than the carbon dioxide. In the Arctic and the Antarctic, there is much less ice than there was in the 1970s. Glaciers are disappearing. And the polar ice caps are part of what keeps the world cool because they're white and they reflect the sunlight back into space. There are a thousand plant and animal species going extinct every week.

The deserts are growing more arid and the storms are shifting the ocean currents. Climate refugees increase. Our children and our grandchildren are the inheritors of all this.

This is the first noble truth in climate change. It's what we have created as human beings on the planet. The first noble truth calls on us to see this clearly.

The second noble truth describes the cause of suffering. The causes are straightforward. Greed, hatred, delusion, and ignorance are the main roots of suffering. You can see the greed in the rapacious way that we treat the natural world. You can see hate in the wars over land, resources, and money. And you can see the deeper delusion, the delusion of separateness. People like to imagine they are separate from the problems, the suffering, but the truth is that every breath you take is shared by the trees, the oceans, by all other life. I've said it before: We are all in this together. The second noble truth of climate change asks us to look at the behavior of corporations and governments, individuals and groups of people. The more greed and hate and fear and delusion, the more we suffer. All these problems are rooted in the human heart.

Fortunately, there is the third noble truth of climate change: Suffering isn't the end of the story. Instead of greed we can live with generosity; instead of hate we can foster love; instead of ignorance we can live with wisdom. The third noble truth shows a new way of being that leads to freedom, care, and healing. There is a release from the struggle. We can choose to turn away from exploitation and fear, mindless competition and climate denial. We will find a collective well-being and a huge peace when we do so.

And last there is the fourth noble truth: There is a path beyond suffering. The path to end suffering asks us to wake up from the trance of separation, from the false sense that we're separate from the rest of it. It invites us to clear seeing and loving understanding. With this realization we can bring all the qualities that we develop in meditation—integrity, seeing the truth, telling the truth, and acting with mindfulness and wise effort—to our way of living. We can turn away from greed and hate. In our business, our governments, and our families, we can shift our focus to foster mutual well-being. We can promote ethical, caring ways of living. We can quiet our minds and open our hearts. We can learn to be loving and present for one another and for the earth itself.

This is the path to well-being and true freedom. Let us walk it together.

Mystery, Death, and Consciousness

Oh Nobly Born,
Remember Who You
Really Are

The powerful play goes on,
and you may contribute a verse.

WALT WHITMAN

THE FOLLOWING STORY, "Nachiketa and the Lord of Death," is part of a series of conversations between a young man and Death. It is found in the Katha Upanishad, one of the most revered and ancient spiritual texts of India.

Nachiketa was a young man who came from a prosperous family in ancient India. As a teenager he became disturbed by the poverty around him. He saw how often the caste system allowed people who were well-off to live by the exploitation of others. They claimed/to be pious but were not. Like many of the young people of today, he saw the hypocrisy of the society around him.

During this time, Nachiketa's wealthy father grew older and became sick. He was increasingly frightened of death and terrified of what was to come. Because Nachiketa's father was anxious about his next reincarnation, he felt concerned about the very worldly way he had lived. He talked to some of his wealthy friends, and they told him to speak with the Brahman priests who ran the biggest temple in the community. To have a good rebirth, the priests explained, he should make a magnificent offering. If he divested himself of everything he owned and offered it to the temple, then he would be given a very fine rebirth. This was shocking news for Nachiketa's father. But the priests held steady. "This will do it!" they assured him.

Nachiketa's father followed their instructions carefully. He created a big public event, complete with a huge parade, for the performance of his donation. And at the culmination of the gathering, he stood at the gates of the temple and said, "I give my cattle, all of my oxen, and all my gold, everything I value, to the priests of this temple." It was a great display.

Nachiketa, his only son, stood there. It struck Nachiketa as truly hypocritical. His father's offering did not have the feeling of genuine spirituality. Very loudly, Nachiketa's father proclaimed, "I give all I value to the temple!"

"What about me, your son?" Nachiketa responded. "Don't you value me?" He said it in a way that was an affront to his father as they were in the middle of the public square during the great celebration.

His father was overcome with anger at being shamed in front of everyone who admired him. He looked at Nachiketa with cold eyes and said, "I give you to death. You are dead to me."

This was devastating for young Nachiketa and he refused to bear it. "I will not go along with this sham," he announced, defiantly.

"Then I give you to death," Nachiketa's father said once more.

"I accept," said Nachiketa. And then he walked away.

Nachiketa wandered for a time, and since his father had given him to death, he sought out Yama, the Lord of Death who presides over the underworld. He knew that he could not continue his old life with his father. Nachiketa went deep into the forest. He took a seat there and vowed, *I will not get up until I see Lord Yama.*

He sat for three days without moving. He withstood great pain and hunger and difficulty. Suddenly, Nachiketa found himself in the kingdom of death. "Where is Lord Yama? I've come to see him," he announced.

"Lord Yama is out collecting rent," his assistants replied. "The only ones here are us, his assistants—War, Pestilence, and Famine. Can we help you?"

Nachiketa shook his head. "No, I will continue to wait for his return." And he waited.

Finally, Lord Yama returned and his assistants told him, "We have a very unusual young man here. Normally people run the other way when they hear you're coming, Lord Yama. But he sat for three days and nights waiting for you, and now he says he will not move until he gets an audience with the Lord of Death."

Lord Yama was curious. He sat down with Nachiketa and gazed at him for a long time.

"You are indeed an unusual young man," said the Lord of Death. "What brings you?"

"I will not live with hypocrisy and injustice," Nachiketa said. "I cannot do that. My father said to me, 'I give you to death.' I told him, 'Then I will go.'"

Listening to this young man, Lord Yama felt sympathy for him. "Because I have kept you waiting for three days," he said, "I will give you three boons, three wishes. What will you choose?"

Nachiketa sat quietly pondering what would support his journey to a new life. After some time, he sensed his first wish. He knew what was needed for him to move on. "I ask for the boon of forgiveness," he said. "May I be forgiven. May my father see me with the eyes that he had for me when I was first born as his son. May all that I have done that's caused pain to others be forgiven. And may I forgive myself."

Nachiketa was not unusual in this regard. We've all been hurt by others. And we have all hurt, betrayed, or abandoned others around us at some point in our lives.

Nachiketa knew to ask for forgiveness, because only forgiveness releases the chains of the heart. Without it, we are not free to move on; we are chained to the past.

Lord Yama obliged. He granted Nachiketa forgiveness.

Now it was time for the second boon. Nachiketa thought again. At last he asked for inner fire, true courage. He said, "May I be granted inner fire, the courage to live my life fully, to truly be alive." Nachiketa knew that when we are courageous, when we are vibrantly alive, all kinds of things are possible. Spiritual practice requires true courage. It helps us to awaken the capacity to be truly alive and present to it all. With this, Lord Yama granted him the inner fire and courage he requested. Then he said, "Young man, I've given you two boons. What do you request for the third one?"

Nachiketa reflected on the deepest possibilities. Finally, he came to the most important request of all: "I ask for that which is immortal, which is undying."

Lord Yama sat back. "Really? You know, you could ask for anything. You could ask for magical powers. You could have a palace. You could have a royal golden chariot. You could have women and consorts. You could have anything! Think it over. This is your last wish! What would be most important for you?"

Nachiketa, being a wise young man, considered this, then looked back at the Lord of Death and said, "Tell me, Lord Yama. All these things you've suggested to me, will they not soon return to your kingdom, return to dust?"

"Well, yes it's true. Yes, they are all temporal," Lord Yama replied.

"Then for my third boon," Nachiketa said, "I request to know that which is beyond death."

With this, Lord Yama said, "I have a gift for you," and he went away for a moment and then returned with a gift that he placed into Nachiketa's hands: a slightly ornate and beautiful mirror. "To know what is beyond death, you must look into this mirror and ask yourself, *Who am I? Who am I? Who am I really?*"

Nachiketa did as he was instructed. He saw his life, the ever-changing circumstances of his moods and thoughts, his relationships, and his changing body. He even saw the end of his body at death. He kept looking beyond all this. What he learned by looking in the mirror was that *he* was the awareness, the consciousness itself asking the question. He was the timeless spirit. That was the reality. That's who he was. Once Nachiketa understood this, his heart became free—free to love, free to forgive, free to remember that he was spirit and not limited by his body or his history. He was filled with love for his family, his community, and all that was alive.

But how could he return carrying this new sense of freedom? Lord Yama sat quietly without a word. And then Nachiketa realized that in the field of love and timeless consciousness, everywhere is holy ground. Miraculously he found himself back in the forest grove. Free in his heart, he turned and walked back into town.

One day when I was sitting quiet and feeling like a motherless child, which I was, it come to me: that feeling of being part of everything, not separate at all. I knew that if I cut a tree, my arm would bleed. And I laughed and I cried and I run all around the house. I knew just what it was. In fact, when it happen, you can't miss it.

ALICE WALKER

"**TELL ME THE WEIGHT** of a snowflake," a small bird, a titmouse, asked a wild dove.

"Nothing more than nothing," was the answer.

"In that case I must tell you a marvelous story," the titmouse said. "I sat on a branch of a fir, close to its trunk, when it began to snow, not heavily, not in a giant blizzard, no, just like in a dream, without any violence. Since I didn't have anything better to do, I counted the snowflakes settling on the twigs and needles of my branch. Their number was exactly 3,741,952. When the next snowflake dropped onto the branch—nothing more than nothing, as you say—the branch broke off."

Having said that, the titmouse flew away. The dove, since Noah's time an authority on change, thought about the story for a while and finally said to herself: "Perhaps there is only one person's voice lacking for peace to come about in the world."[1]

There is only one world; the world pressing against you at this minute. There is only one minute in which you are alive; this minute here and now. The only way to live is by accepting each minute as an unrepeatable miracle.

STORM JAMESON

I am not I.
   I am this one
walking beside me whom I do not see,
whom at times I manage to visit,
and whom at other times I forget;
the one who remains silent while I talk,
the one who forgives, sweet, when I hate,
the one who takes a walk when I am indoors,
the one who will remain standing when I die.

            JUAN RAMÓN JIMÉNEZ[2]

CONGESTIVE HEART FAILURE put my father into the Hospital of the University of Pennsylvania, and I flew to Philadelphia to sit with him. He had been a difficult father. At times violent, paranoid, and a wife batterer. Yes, he was a brilliant scientist who designed some of the first artificial hearts and lungs and worked in space medicine. But his mental problems were equally large. Now lying there weak and worried, every few minutes he would strain to look up at the heart monitor to see if he was still alive.

As a biophysicist he understood such instruments and hoped somehow this would save him. I had sat with many people as they died, but he was my father. This was different. I sat with him for some days, and every night, when it had grown late, and I was ready to return to my hotel room, he would say, "Please stay, don't go." He was terrified. His prognosis was dire.

I asked him what he thought happened when you died.

"Nothing. You return to dirt," he said bitterly. As a scientist and a materialist, he believed that the body was all we are.

In a lull between nursing visits and beeping machines, I said, "Let me tell you something different about death." I told him about the first time I had an out-of-body experience. I'd been sitting for twenty hours a day in a Burmese monastery. Exhausted, I lay down on the floor to sleep, determined to get up in twenty minutes. I got up and slowly walked to the window at the far end of my narrow cottage. I looked out across the monastery grounds and could see my teacher in the distance, sitting outside speaking with another student. Then I turned around and walked very slowly in the other direction and stopped short.

There was my body lying on the floor asleep. I was so intent on getting up that I did. Just not in my body. I stood over my body for a time, gazing down, and when I relaxed, I fell into my body on the floor and my eyes opened. I walked over to the window and sure enough there was my teacher sitting speaking with the student as I had observed. This was the first of a number of out-of-body experiences I have experienced. They most commonly happen spontaneously. People leave their body during accidents or surgery, but you can also train to have out-of-body moments in meditation.

After this, I told my father about my experiences sitting with people who were dying and how sometimes they would leave their body and appear clinically dead, or near death, and then return with stories of light and peace and joy and excitement. I also explained how I remembered a past life in meditation. Then I described the past life regressions I had led for years and shared about how often people who did not believe in past lives had remarkable experiences. Especially when I directed them to go back to a lifetime that had an important lesson related to this current life.

My father looked skeptical. But this was his nature about everything.

Still, I carried on. I told him that when he died, everything would become peaceful. He would feel himself floating out of his body. There would be a sense of lightness and freedom and likely some light. This can often be a time of reflection, I told him, where people look back at their whole life's incarnation, with understanding and love.

"Do you believe this is possible?" I finally asked him.

He slowly shook his head no.

"Well," I replied, "you are a scientist, so you have to wait and see." I paused and laughed and said, "And if it happens, remember, I told you so!"

Two days after he died, I was still in Philadelphia, and he came to me in a dream. I opened the door where my mother and brothers and I were all staying and saw him standing there as if waiting to come in. I told him I was glad to see him, but was surprised as well, since he had died.

"I died?" he asked, and his face looked confused and quizzical.

"Yes, you died," I said.

He stared at me for a few moments, looking wistful.

Then he slowly turned and faded as he walked quietly away.

IN TIMES OF MAJOR CHANGES, we are initiated into something new. Initiation is a language that honors and reframes the difficulties that we go through. Initiation comes in many forms: loss, divorce, the death of loved ones, illness, challenges. It is at times described "as a narrow passage that's difficult to get through." You can't take your old identity with you. Initiation strips you down in some difficult way.

Sometimes we choose to go through the initiation. We can put ourselves through a challenging experience that will ripen and transform us. We can take that leap—and trust the person we will become on the other side. A part of us will die, and a new part will be born.

More often, initiation comes unbidden. We receive what in Greek is called a katabas, a blow or a crisis that comes when we are going along with our routine and all of a sudden something happens that entirely changes our life. It happens to all of us, and when it happens, it forces us to step out of the ordinary way that we are moving along in life. It calls on us to deepen and learn something new in that crisis. It asks for a profound letting go. When we survive it, we become more of an initiated person, someone seasoned, wiser, more sturdy, less afraid. Initiation brings us alive in a new way and hopefully makes us more compassionate toward each other.

Inside the Great Mystery that is,
we don't really own anything.
What is this competition we feel then,
before we go, one at a time, through the same gate?

RUMI

When we feel the brevity of life,
    the commonplace becomes precious:
A cup of tea
the luminous gold of a sunset,
a maple tree in autumn,
the laughter of a child,
the gaze of a beloved.

I recommend almost dying to everyone.
It's character building. You get a much clearer
perspective of what's important and what
isn't, the preciousness and beauty of life.

CARL SAGAN

SEVERAL YEARS AGO, I was called to visit a man in a San Francisco hospital. He was in his late thirties and already wealthy from the major construction company that he built. He owned a big sailboat, a vast ranch, a town house, and a place in Aspen. One day when driving along in his fancy BMW, he blacked out. Tests showed that he had a brain tumor, a rapid-growing cancer. The doctor said, "We want to operate on you, but I must warn you that the tumor is in the speech and comprehension center. If we remove the tumor, you may lose all of your ability to read, to write, to speak, or to understand any language. If we don't operate, you probably have six more weeks to live. Please consider this. We want to operate in the morning. Let us know by then."

I visited this man that evening. He had become very quiet and reflective. As you can imagine, he was in an extraordinary state of consciousness. Such an awakening will sometimes come from our spiritual practice, but for him it came through these exceptional circumstances. When we spoke, this man did not talk about his ranch or his sailboat or his money. Where he was headed, they don't take the currency of bankbooks and jets. All that is of value in times of great change is the currency of our heart—the abilities and understandings of the heart that have grown in us.

In his early twenties, this man had done a little Zen meditation and had read a bit of Alan Watts, and when he faced this moment, that is what he drew on and what he wanted to talk about: his spiritual life and understanding of birth and death. After a heartfelt conversation, he paused to be silent for a time and reflect. Finally he turned to me and said, "I've had enough of talking. Maybe I've said too many words. This evening our life seems so precious. I am touched just to have a drink of tap water or to watch the pigeons on the windowsill of the medical center fly off in the air. They seem so beautiful to me. It's magic to see a bird go through the air. I'm not finished. Maybe I'll just have to live more silently."

So he asked to have the operation. After fourteen hours of surgery by a very fine surgeon, his sister visited him in the recovery room. He looked up at her and said, "Good morning." They had been able to remove the tumor without him losing his ability to speak.

When he left the hospital and recovered from his cancer, his entire life changed. He still completed his business obligations, but he was no longer a workaholic. He spent time with his family, and he became a beloved counselor and support for others diagnosed with cancer and grave illnesses. He spent much of his time in nature and much of his time touching the people around him with love.[3]

In the midst of winter, I found there was,
within me, an invincible summer.

ALBERT CAMUS

WHEN THINGS ARE truly difficult, and people consider taking their own life, very often they're right about needing to die. But there's a profound mistake in their wish. They think their body has to die, when in fact it is something else. There is something in their life that needs to die. It might be a difficult role they've taken on that does not suit their spirit. It could be the wrong job or the untrue identity they have lived. It could be that they haven't come out of the closet—or the closet itself needs to die. It might be a marriage that doesn't work. It might be shame. Or great guilt or grief or loss or a financial crisis that they feel they can't face. But we are survivors. With surrender and help, we can pass through it.

When we think it is our body that needs to die, it is a call for facing a different kind of death. Throughout our lives, there are times when something needs to die in order for us to become bigger.

MY COLLEAGUE Michelle McDonald was a preschool teacher, and one day she said to her class, "Let's learn about death." Little kids know about death. Death is hard to miss because it is all around us; children see it too.

Michelle asked the children to go out in the forest and collect dead things. They found dry, decomposing leaves, old tree bark, and dead bare sticks. Somebody found a part of a skeleton of a mouse or a lizard. Once she called them back inside, they made a whole pile of dead things. And then they began to talk about it.

What is death?

Why do things die?

Then she asked them, "What would happen if there wasn't death?"

One little girl raised her hand. "Well, then there'd be more and more trees and there'd be no room for us! Everything would get too crowded," she said.

Even children can see this truth: We are all part of a cycle. We can trust this. We are always dying and being reborn in new ways. What dies makes way for something new to come in.

I lived for thousands of years as a mineral,
and then died and became a plant.
And I lived for thousands of years as a plant,
and then died and became an animal.
And I lived for thousands of years as an animal,
and then died and became a human being.
Tell me, what have I ever lost by dying?

            RUMI

I asked the leaf whether it was frightened because it was autumn and the other leaves were falling. The leaf told me, "No. During the whole spring and summer I was completely alive. I worked hard to help nourish the tree, and now much of me is in the tree. I am not limited by this form. I am also the whole tree, and when I go back to the soil, I will continue to nourish the tree. So I don't worry at all. As I leave this branch and float to the ground, I will wave to the tree and tell her, 'I will see you again very soon.'" That day there was a wind blowing and, after a while, I saw the leaf leave the branch and float down to the soil, dancing joyfully, because as it floated it saw itself already there in the tree. It was so happy. I bowed my head, knowing that I have a lot to learn from the leaf because it is not afraid—it knew nothing can be born and nothing can die.

THICH NHAT HANH

I HAD TRAVELED TO WORK with my beloved friend Maha Ghosananda in the Cambodian refugee camps. After the Khmer Rouge genocide, only parts of families had survived—a mother and three children, an old uncle and two nephews—and in the crowded camps each was given a little bamboo hut about four feet wide, six feet long, and five feet high. In front of each hut was a little patch of land perhaps no bigger than one square yard. After a few months of camp life, next to most of the huts in their little squares of ground, people had planted gardens. They would have a squash plant with two or three small squash on it, or a bean plant, or some other vegetable. The plants were very carefully tended, with little bamboo stakes for support. The tendrils of a bean plant would wind around the stake and up over the roof of the house.

Every day each refugee family would walk a mile and stand for half an hour in a long line at the pit well at the far end of the camp and carry back a bucket of water for their plants. It was a touching and beautiful thing to see these gardens in the middle of this camp in the dry season, when you could barely believe that anything would grow on such a hot barren field.

As these war-shattered families planted and watered their tiny gardens, they awakened the unstoppable force of life. So can we! No matter what inner difficulty or suffering we may experience, in taking the one seat and in tending to all that arises with compassionate awareness, we will discover this same unstoppable life force.

Though I do not believe that a plant will spring up where no seed has been, I have great faith in a seed. Convince me that you have a seed there, and I am prepared to expect wonders.

HENRY DAVID THOREAU

This body is not me.
I am not limited by this body.
I am life without boundaries.
I have never been born,
and I have never died.

Look at the ocean and the sky filled with stars,
manifestations from my wondrous true mind.
Since before time, I have been free.

Birth and death are only doors through which we pass,
sacred thresholds on our journey.
Birth and death are a game of hide-and-seek.

So laugh with me,
hold my hand,
let us say good-bye,
say good-bye, to meet again soon.

We meet today.
We will meet again tomorrow.
We will meet at the source every moment.
We meet each other in all forms of life.

        THICH NHAT HANH[4]

Wisdom tells me I am nothing.
Love tells me I am everything.
And between the two my life flows.

NISARGADATTA MAHARAJ

AT THE END OF OUR three-month retreat at the Insight Meditation Society, we invited visiting teachers to speak to the students. After three months of silent meditation, everyone was calm and very open. A famous Korean Zen master from the nine mountains monasteries came and was told the students had been practicing hard for months. But when he joined them and looked at everyone, he said, "Oh, no good. You are not really practicing."

The meditators were shocked, but of course that's what good Zen masters do.

Then the master continued, "Not just mindfulness. Not that. Only one thing." Then he took his stick and banged it on the floor. As he banged it, he said, "What is this? What is this?" Then he shouted, "What is this life? This life, this body? You must answer!"

It was a powerful moment, even though everyone was shaking. The Zen master had pointed them to the most important question: Who are you?

The intensity of the question shocked these quiet students into a state of mystery, of questioning everything. It brought a state of wonderment.

When we question deeply, there is no ground, no place to stand—just an amazement that life exists and that consciousness exists to know it.

Conscious awareness doesn't age. You are not your changing thoughts. You're not your waves of emotions. Even though they're very dramatic and can be appreciated, they pass.

So what are you? You are consciousness, you are loving awareness itself. Consciousness goes through the adventures of life and forgets its true nature.

And then, in a moment, we wake up and remember our life is like a dream, an echo, a rainbow ... Our human incarnation in this world of form needs to be honored and loved fully.

But in the end it is all insubstantial. Knowing this, we can live well and be unafraid, even when it's time for death.

When a baby is born they think,
"Do not let me forget who I really am."
But soon after, "Oh, I am forgetting already."

INDIAN SAYING

THE MORE YOU ALLOW YOURSELF to see your life as a series of initiations large and small, the more you begin to trust rebirth itself. The great chemist Antoine Lavoisier explained, "In nature, nothing is created, nothing is lost, everything is transformed." When you look at the equations of chemistry, you see that molecules never disappear completely. They change; they go into a new compound. But nothing is lost. This is a spiritual truth as well.

When you go through hard things, trust that although you lose things that you love, people you care about, and the way things were, there will come something new on the other side of it. It's not the end of the story. You are living through the cycle of birth and death that happens all the time.

Change is our life, every day. The nature of existence is ceaseless transformation. Every day you're reborn; every morning you are new at breakfast. And just as our individual lives change, so does the collective. We live in an age of tremendous cultural anxiety, where suffering and pain is inflicted on large numbers of the most vulnerable in the communities and in the world. We need to respond, but it is also true that the difficulties will shift. It's inevitable that something new will be born; we just don't know what it is. Our job is to lovingly tend and plant benevolent seeds so that whatever is compassionate, new, and good may happen.

Death OK. Rebirth OK too.

JOSHU SASAKI ROSHI

THERE IS AN ANCIENT TEXT called the Mahāparinibbāna Sutta that recounts in detail the whole last year of the Buddha's life. It begins in an almost mythological way, saying, "Once upon a time," and it unfolds with many questions as well as answers. You can follow along in this story.

❊

In ancient India, when tigers roamed the forests and the land was verdant and wild, the Buddha, near the end of his life, decided to travel north to his birthplace in the foothills of the Himalayas, knowing he was soon to enter nirvana, a state of ultimate peace. Along the way, he settled for a time in a tranquil grove of trees on Vulture's Peak. The air was thick with the fragrance of blooming flowers, and the hearts of his followers were heavy but brimming with reverence. There, the Buddha's attendant came to him to announce a visitor.

The chief minister of one of the local kings had come with an important question: Should we make war on the Vajjians? The Vajjians were enemies of this minister's kingdom.

The Buddha reflected for a moment before he replied. He often did not give direct answers, preferring to elicit understanding through a series of questions: "Do the Vajjians meet regularly in harmony? Do they treat one another with respect? Do they listen to one another with care? If they do, they can be expected to prosper and not decline. And do they follow the wise traditions of the ancestors and elders and great teachers? If they do, they can be expected to prosper and not decline. Do they take care of the vulnerable among them—the women, the children, those who are vulnerable in other ways? If they do, they will prosper and not decline. And do they take care of the natural environment and the sacredness of nature around them? If they do, they can be expected to prosper and not decline."

Then the Buddha elaborated, explaining to the minister that if you care for the sick and the vulnerable in your community, if you treat your temples and dwelling places with respect and care, if you preserve your personal mindfulness, and if the spiritual leaders, both in public and in private, show lovingkindness and respect to those around them in acts of body, speech, mind, and heart, then all will be well. When he was done speaking, the minister bowed and thanked him for the wise guidance. Given the Buddha's answer, he knew they should not make war against the Vajjian people.

You might wonder, why the Buddha didn't just say that war is bad and that it is wrong to kill people. He chose to offer teachings that pointed the minister to a deeper truth: how the law of cause and effect governs life. If you have a just society where people treat each other well, then the fruits of that will be peace and strength in the community. The way you live with one another and how you treat each other and the world around you will create the world that you live in and will make a steady, strong community.

❁

After this visit the Buddha began traveling again with his group of monastics. Following a few days of walking, they stopped in a mango grove. Sariputra, the wisest of the Buddha's disciples, sat down with the Buddha and with tremendous love and respect in his heart said, "There has never been a more enlightened teacher than you in this world. You are the best. There's never been anybody as wise and as wonderful as you."

The Buddha looked at him and said, "Sariputra, how can you make a statement like this? Do you know all the Buddhas past and future? Do you know all the great teachers of the world?"

Sariputra, undeterred in his wisdom, replied, "It is as if there's a great city and to protect it from marauders and all things that could harm the inhabitants, there is only one gate. And at this one gate there is a guard who can see what is skillful and helpful to those who inhabit the city. The guard can also see what is dangerous. He sees with great clarity and lives in a completely present and mindful way. The guard allows what's useful to come in and keeps what's not useful out. The gate is the reality of the present moment and the guard is mindfulness. Mindfulness and clarity are the abode of all Buddhas and awakened ones."

The Buddha smiled and said, "Just so Sariputra."

When we stay mindful like the guard, present with kindness and discernment to whatever arises, then all things get tended well. Presence and freedom are found here and now.

❊

As the days passed, the Buddha continued to head north with his company of followers. A warm and wet wind announced that soon they would come to the banks of the Ganges River. When they arrived, they sat on its shore. The Buddha said to those around him, "Followers, I have offered to you teachings to cross the flood. A boat, a raft. These teachings allow you to leave the shores of suffering, fear, and separateness. You can cross the flood to a place of inner freedom of heart, no matter the changing conditions, dwelling in liberation and compassion. And friends, once you've crossed the river, would it be useful to carry the boat or the raft with you?"

The monks and nuns responded, "No, Venerable One."

"Just so, my friends," the Buddha said. "Use these teachings as a raft to move from the shore of entanglement and fear to the realm of liberation. But do not be attached to them. Don't carry them; only use them for freedom."

The Buddha recognized how people who follow spiritual teachings don't know how to put the raft down. He saw how people cling to their raft or fight about their boats with other people. They just need to put the boat down.

❧

Days passed, and the Buddha and his followers carried on again. When he grew tired, the Buddha went to sit quietly in the forest under a great tree. And as he quietly sat, Mara, the god who personifies suffering, greed, hatred, ignorance, and fear, appeared. He had visited the Buddha many times before, throwing all sorts of temptations at the Buddha. Under the Bodhi tree, Mara had unleashed his armies of anger, aversion, and hatred onto the Buddha. But always, every single time, the Buddha had held steady. But here, even in Buddha's last days, he had come again. Maybe at the end of his life, the Buddha would be weakened, but when Mara approached, the Buddha did not move. "Oh, I see you, Mara," he said. "Here you are again."

"What right do you have to sit here?" Mara asked.

The Buddha reached down and touched the earth and said, "As I've said to you before, the earth is my witness that I have offered my whole life and countless lifetimes out of compassion and care for the beings of this world. I have a right to awaken, as does every human being."

"When I challenged you in the past, you vowed to teach others to awaken. Now you have completed your life's tasks: May the Blessed One take final nirvana," Mara said. He would then bother him no longer.

"Mara, you need not worry," the Buddha replied. "I see you. It's not long. Several months more and I will release this eighty-year-old body. It is worn out. This time I'll go along with you because in several months it will be my time."

Even in the end, the Buddha was kind to Mara. The Buddha knew we all need Mara in order to become enlightened. Mara comes to test us all. We live in a world where there is love and connection and the timeless truth of freedom, but there's also separateness and fear and confusion. It is only by including both sides that the seed of liberation can grow.

No mud, no lotus. No Mara, no Buddha.

Overcoming Mara was part of the dance of the Buddha's awakening. Because of Mara, we are given the opportunity to have a different relationship with the difficulties of life. Difficulties are part of the fabric of life. The Buddha had always been one to respect Mara.

As soon as the Buddha said yes to Mara, as soon as he acknowledged he would soon die and would take his final nirvana in the next months, a hair-raising earthquake shook the earth. Ananda, the Buddha's beloved attendant, came running to the tree where the Buddha sat.

"What is this earthquake?" Ananda cried.

"There are many causes for earthquakes," the Buddha said. "There's the natural earthquake, but also there's the earthquake when a Buddha is born and the one when a Buddha gets enlightened and there is another when a Buddha dies. But this particular quake came because I told Mara it is my time."

Ananda could not deny this truth. Mara's final visit and the Buddha's acknowledgment of his coming death were earth-shaking events, profound happenings that would ripple across all space and time. Yet still, Ananda got very upset and began to weep. He said to the Buddha, "Oh, how many times you've said you could live a long time! You said you would live a century. Please don't die yet; please live for a hundred years!"

"My body is now like an old cart held together with straps and ropes," the Buddha replied. "It is time. I must take my nirvana in a few months."

"But you said you could live for a century!" Ananda said.

"Yes, but yours is the fault, Ananda," the Buddha said. "I gave you hints over these last years in the black snake pool, in Jivaka's mango grove, and in Deer Park. If you had asked me three times to please live for a century, then I could have. If you'd asked just two times, I would've demurred no. But on the third time,

I would've had to say yes. I would've lived for a hundred years. Yours is the fault."

Ananda, the Buddha's most beloved attendant, felt for a moment like a great failure. He'd ignored these hints.

Why ever would the Buddha say this to his dear Ananda?

Finally, Ananda understood the teaching behind it. The teacher-student relationship has never been, and never will be, one way. Nothing is up to one person. He, too, had a responsibility. The Buddha was saying to him, his most caring and loving of attendants, "Ananda, it's up to our relationship with one another. Even as the Buddha, I need you, just as you need me, to care for the Dharma. The responsibility of awakening is not just in the hand of the teacher. It is in the hands of all of us who practice."

❖

A month passed, and the Buddha's time was now closer. Eventually the Buddha got up and continued to walk, and as he wandered, visitors continued to come and ask questions and get teachings. And as he gave teachings, he would respond to the people around him with love and wisdom, and their hearts would open and their minds become vast. He invited a state of freedom beyond their small separate sense of self. Those who understood became filled with compassion for the whole world.

With each person, the Buddha ended by saying, "Now it is time for you to do as you see fit," pointing each person toward themselves and to the possibility of liberation that lived within their heart. This is and will always be the birthright of all of us.

His followers knew they had to awaken themselves. The Buddha placed it in their hands, a true moment of empowerment.

"No one can let go for you. No one can awaken for you. No one can love for you," the Buddha said.

"Then who will be our guide?" Ananda asked.

"The Dharma, the teachings, will be your guide," the Buddha said. "I will not put another person in charge of the community. Let the truth and the teachings themselves be your guides. Be an island unto yourself. Take these teachings with your own responsibility.

"Those who do not live with attention to their words and deeds, who don't act out of kindness and respect, will lose their wealth and will lose their reputation. They will lose sleep and die confused." He did not mince words.

"But on the other hand," he said, "if you pay attention to your life and live with dignity and care and respect for living beings, then there comes honor and health and well-being and ease of sleep. And your death comes naturally in its appropriate time and with ease."

"How will we know that we are following the right Dharma, the right teachings? What are the true teachings of the Buddha?" a monk asked.

"It might be that you hear them from the lips of the another. It might be that the community of followers say, 'These are the real teachings.' It might be said by a circle of learned elders. It might be a master. None of these will tell you for sure what the correct teachings are. You cannot rely on any of these. Instead, if what you hear conforms to the essence and the gist of what I have shared with you about freedom and the awakened heart, about the path of virtue, meditation, and lovingkindness, then you know it is the Dharma. Compassion and lovingkindness should grow in you through the practices and understandings I have given you. The true teachings show you that attachment and grasping lead to fear, confusion, and suffering and that you can free yourself from this grasping. If what you hear conforms with the heart of these, then you know you are following the right way."

✽

The Buddha had just a few days of walking in him left. Followed by a very large retinue, he was slowing down. The travel was difficult, but his heart was at peace. He and his followers came to rest in a forest grove, where the Buddha was approached by a courtesan, Ambapali, dressed in the finest silks and perfumes. When she arrived at the edge of the forest grove, she got out of her carriage and walked over to the Buddha to pay her respects and tell him of the beautiful sense of awakening that the Buddha had touched in her.

She said to him, "I have shifted from being confused and closed to open and free in my heart and mind. Will the Buddha and his company of followers come and take a meal at my home?"

"Yes," the Buddha said, without hesitation.

Shortly after, a group of nobles, and princes began to arrive behind the courtesan. Their royal carts were dressed in magnificent blue, yellow, and white silks and adornments, and they had many horses and elephants. When they saw Ambapali, they whispered behind her back and insulted her with their glances. "Oh my, this mango woman got here before us," they said. Then they too invited the Buddha to their palaces to give teachings. But the Buddha politely declined.

"Thank you for the invitation," he said. "I've already accepted the invitation of Ambapali. I cannot come."

"Oh no. Oh no!" they said, pleading. They raced after her and offered her a hundred thousand pieces of gold so that she might give up her time with the Buddha. But Ambapali kept to her invitation. "Not for a whole kingdom would I give up this invitation to make offerings to the Blessed One and have him come to receive our offering." The Buddha then followed Ambapali to where she and her courtesans dwelled.

Even though the Buddha was of princely birth, he honored Ambapali's request. He made it clear that practices of awakening are not just for nobles and princes. Everyone can practice and everyone can awaken. In the eyes of the Buddha, no one was higher or lower. Everyone is nobly born.

"Remember who you are," he said to his followers that day. "You're not this small separate self. You, all of you, are endowed with awareness itself, and the possibility of freedom is there for every single one of you. Whoever comes with a good heart, that's the noble person."

❀

When the Buddha left his host Ambapali, he wandered once more until he came to a small village. There, a smith offered the Buddha his last meal, which the Buddha accepted.

"Give the other food to my followers. I'll take the special food that you have prepared for me," the Buddha said. Then he told the smith that great blessings and merit come to those who give the first meal to the Buddha after his enlightenment and those who give the last meal to the Buddha at the end of his life.

"You are that person," the Buddha said to the smith.

And it just so happened that the meal the smith gave to him was spoiled. The smith did not know this. Not long after eating, the Buddha got terribly sick with dysentery. Soon he would die from this very meal. The smith was devastated—but quickly, the Buddha reassured him. The Buddha knew that nobody else should eat that one spoiled plate. He knew it was his time.

And he made it clear that the smith would receive much merit because what mattered was the motivation in the heart of the person who offered it to him. It was the intention that mattered. The smith's offering was steeped in purity. The key to merit, and the key to karma, is the motivation behind things. If you have a truly caring heart and wise intentions, you will plant the seed for something good to happen, even if it takes that seed a long time to bear fruit.

※

After the meal, the Buddha sat with his weakened body by the edge of a river. A train of five hundred merchant carts came by. With the carts came an enormous thunderstorm, making the river run thick with dirt and silt from the carts and the mountainside in the distance. "Ananda, I want a cup of water," the Buddha said.

"But the river is all stirred up by the carts in the rainstorm," Ananda replied.

"Please get me a cup of water," he said again.

Ananda, uncertain, went to the river to fetch a cupful. And as he stood at its shore, he saw that the river was magically now completely clear. The water he brought to the Buddha was beautiful, and the Buddha drank from it.

A wandering yogi, who watched it happen, was astounded. "I've never seen anything like this!" he exclaimed. "How did you do this?"

It came down to a simple truth: The water reflected the purity of the Buddha's heart. There is a reality that is completely clear and pure. A timeless reality that can't be touched by the circumstances of the world. In all of our hearts and spirits, with wise understanding, there is to be found an untouchable and unshakeable purity and goodness.

After this a devout follower came to see the Buddha by the river. He brought an offering: a set of golden robes. When the Buddha put the robes around himself, his own skin began to glow with a golden light. But why gold? Gold is a metal that can never tarnish. In the same way that the river reflected his purity, the glowing skin of the Buddha shone outward a state of glowing compassion for the whole world, a liberated heart and mind that is untarnished by changing conditions.

❖

The time had arrived. The Buddha was in great pain. Illness had taken over his bodily form. And so the Buddha lay down in the lion's pose on his right side between two Sal trees, which immediately went into bloom. Angels and devas circled around the trees, and they shined their eyes and their light down on the Blessed One.

Everything was radiant. Even in death, even in the midst of the most difficult circumstances, his vibrant and pure spirit was there.

"Don't die here," Ananda, his attendant, said. "This is a miserable backwater town, a daub and wattle village. This is not a proper place for the Blessed One to die."

"Do not call this a miserable backwater," the Buddha said.

"But you should go to Varanasi, or somewhere great. Die there. Make it a good death. Somewhere magnificent," Ananda pleaded.

"Do not call it a miserable backwater," the Buddha said again. "Once upon a time long ago in this very spot lived in ancient monarch, a wheel-turning monarch, a righteous king. And his kingdom, well populated, was a kingdom of justice for all, full of the sounds of elephants and carriages, gongs and commerce and cattle, and full of joys. And the great roads from his palace stretched out in each of the four directions. I was that king, and I will die here.

"Remember, Ananda, any place can be the kingdom of righteousness. When the mind becomes silent and the heart becomes vast, exactly where you are is the place of liberation. This place can never be found in the physical world. Wherever you are, when the heart is pure and the eyes are open to see this world with compassion and freedom, that is the place of awakening."

❊

One final visitor came to see the Buddha.

"No more, no," said Ananda. "The Buddha cannot accept any more visitors. He's getting ready to die."

"Let him come in, let him come in," said the Buddha, still open-handed. "Everyone is welcome. The Dharma is for everyone; the teachings are never secrets. I've given you everything you need. I've reminded you of everything you must know to awaken your own heart and mind. Let this man come in, whoever he is. Let me give my teachings to him as well."

After this the Buddha looked around and said, "Does anybody have any doubts? Have I not taught you well? Is there some question you have? Have I shown the way to liberation, to not cling to this world, to step out of the small sense of self, of fear and confusion, and rest in the liberated heart?"

No one had questions.

"Then be of good resolve, all of you, in the dispensation of the Buddha. For if you practice wisely, the earth will never be free of enlightened beings. Remember, all created things are impermanent; they all change. Be a lamp, a light unto yourself; find your freedom."

And then the Buddha closed his eyes and went into deep meditation. And at some point, death took him.

Some of the monks and followers wept; some tore their hair out. "Oh, the Blessed One is gone," they cried. The more awakened ones said, "Listen, didn't he just teach you that everything's impermanent? Why is the grief here and why are you complaining? The Buddha just told us not to be attached." But still, the others wept. In the end, those around him showed all the sides of our humanity.

A great funeral was held. His followers made a big stupa and treated his remains like that of a king. Five hundred layers of linen and cotton and perfume covered his body. But when it came time to light the fire they could not do so, because one of the great disciples of the Buddha was still walking there with five hundred monks and nuns. No matter how much they tried, the fire wouldn't light. But once the disciple arrived and laid his head at the foot of the Buddha, the fire spontaneously lit. And then an earthquake shook the earth beneath them. Flowers rained down from the heavens to celebrate and honor the life of the great awakened one.

❈

"Make of yourself a light,"
said the Buddha,
before he died.
I think of this every morning
as the east begins
to tear off its many clouds
of darkness, to send up the first
signal—a white fan
streaked with pink and violet,
even green.
An old man, he lay down
between two sala trees,
and he might have said anything,
knowing it was his final hour.
The light burns upward,
it thickens and settles over the fields.
Around him, the villagers gathered

and stretched forward to listen.
Even before the sun itself
hangs, disattached, in the blue air,
I am touched everywhere
by its ocean of yellow waves.
No doubt he thought of everything
that had happened in his difficult life.
And then I feel the sun itself
as it blazes over the hills,
like a million flowers on fire—
clearly I'm not needed,
yet I feel myself turning
into something of inexplicable value.
Slowly, beneath the branches,
he raised his head.
He looked into the faces of that frightened crowd.

MARY OLIVER[5]

Make of yourself a light.

PRACTICE

You Are Consciousness

Human consciousness has the capacity to open us up to a vastness far beyond our usual small sense of self. In a transcendent moment, you can tap in to it. Maybe it happens when you are looking at the evening stars on a dark night in the desert. It might happen when you are listening to an amazing piece of music. Or making love. Or when you witness the birth of a child. It can happen when you are holding the hand of someone as they die, as their spirit leaves their body. It is a powerful moment, huge and yet silent like a falling star.

When the gates between the worlds open, all of a sudden you say to yourself, "Wow, what *is* this life? What is this life for? What is this?" In those moments, you can see that you are not just this body. Your body changes. You were once a little tiny baby body, then you moved into your kid body, then you had the body of an adult. But that's not you. You are not kale and hamburgers. You rent your body. You get to use it for a little while. But truthfully, you are the spirit that was born into your body and that will leave it.

What does it mean to remember that who you are is actually consciousness itself? To rest in vastness. Try it.

Close your eyes. Then try to sense the spirit that came into your body. Loving awareness is who you are.

Here is one way to do this: Begin by sitting quietly. Listen to all the sounds that arise as you sit. Take your time. Some are soft, some are loud, some are nearby, and some are distant. As you listen, let yourself imagine, sense, feel, or pretend that your mind can open far beyond the size of your head. Sense that it is like open space, an awareness as wide as the sky. Notice how even the most distant sounds are heard arising and passing in the vast space of your mind. All the sounds are arising and passing like clouds. Then notice how sensations, thoughts, images, and emotions, just like sounds, all arise and pass. The mind is not limited by whatever arises. Mindful loving awareness is big enough to hold the whole dance of life: the joys and the sorrows, the gain and the loss, the pleasure and the pain, the beauty and the ocean of tears.

You are larger than you think. When you understand this, you are free.

Rest in vastness.

Freedom comes when you can sit in meditation and allow the whole range of story and emotion—the longing and the love and the tenderness and the fear—and say, "Yes, all this can be held in compassion and the space of loving awareness."

You become vast.

And free.

Rest in timeless awareness. This is who you really are.

Notes

The Respectful Heart

1. Anthony de Mello, *The Prayer of the Frog*, vol. 2 (Gujarat Sahitya Prakash, 2003).
2. Jack Kornfield, adapted excerpt from *A Path with Heart: A Guide Through the Perils and Promises of Spiritual Life*. Copyright © 1993 by Jack Kornfield. Used by permission of Bantam Books, an imprint and division Penguin Random House, LLC. All rights reserved.
3. Originally published in Sakyong Mipham, *Turning the Mind Into an Ally* (Riverhead Books, 2003), 3-4.
4. Dan Baum, "Battle Lessons," *New Yorker*, January 9, 2005.
5. Story originally published in Jack Kornfield, *A Lamp in the Darkness: Illuminating the Path Through Difficult Times*, rev. ed. (Sounds True, 2014), 29-30. Revised for retelling in this book.

Generosity of Vision

1. Mary Oliver, "What Can I Say" from *Swan: Poems and Prose Poems* (Beacon Press, 2010). Reprinted by the permission of The Charlotte Sheedy Literary Agency as agent for the Estate of the author. Copyright © 2010 by Mary Oliver with permission of Bill Reichblum.
2. Rick Fields, "The Very Short Sutra on the Meeting of the Buddha and the Goddess" from *Dharma Gaia: A Harvest of Essays in Buddhism and Ecology*, edited by Allan Hunt-Badiner. Copyright © 1995 by Rick Fields. Reprinted with the permission of Marcia Fields.
3. Story originally published in Jack Kornfield, *A Wise Heart: A Guide to the Universal Teachings of Buddhist Psychology* (Sounds True, 2008). Revised for retelling in this book.
4. Story originally published in Jack Kornfield, ed., *Teachings of the Buddha* (Shambhala Publications, 2024). Revised for retelling in this book.
5. Michael Levenson, "A Gay Couple in Natick Was Targeted. Here's How the Neighborhood Responded," *Boston Globe*, August 22, 2016.
6. Susan Griffin, "Can the Imagination Save Us?" *The Tyee*, November 15, 2004, thetyee.ca/Citizentoolkit/2004/11/15/CanImagSaveUs/.
7. Sanjay Gupta, "Dr. Sanja Gupta: Lessons from Meditating with the Dalai Lama," CNN, cnn.com/2017/02/15/health/sanjay-gupta-dalai-lama-meditation/index.html.

8. Thomas Merton, *Conjectures of a Guilty Bystander* (Penguin Random House Christian Publishing, 2009).
9. Richard Selzer, *Mortal Lessons: Notes on the Art of Surgery* (Simon and Schuster, 1976).
10. Karlfried Graf Durckheim, *The Way of Transformation: Daily Life as Spiritual Practice* (Morning Light Press, 2006), 107–108.
11. "The Cellist of Sarajevo," *World Tribune* (January 10, 2025): 10, worldtribune.org/2025/the-cellist-of-sarajevo/.
12. Laszlo Slomovits, "Strangers" from *Rattle 60* (Summer, 2018). Reprinted with the permission of the author.
13. Story originally published in Joseph Goldstein and Jack Kornfield, *Seeking the Heart of Wisdom: The Path of Insight Meditation* (Shambhala Publications, 1987), 212–13. Revised for retelling in this book.
14. Adapted from Thich Nhat Hanh, *No Death, No Fear: Comforting Wisdom for Life* (Riverhead Books, 2003), 174–75.
15. Sandra Yi, "Boy Who Received Thousands of Books Shares the Wealth," *Deseret News*, September 17, 2015, deseret.com/2015/7/26/20569091/sandy-mailman-s-plea-for-books-gets-worldwide-response/.

Healing and Freedom

1. Richard Selzer, excerpt from "The Surgeon as Priest" from *Mortal Lessons: Notes on the Art of Surgery*. Copyright © 1974, 1975, 1976, 1987 by Richard Selzer. Used

by permission of Georges Borchardt, Inc. on behalf of the author's estate.
2. Ram Dass and Paul Gorman, *How Can I Help? Stories and Reflections on Service* (Alfred A. Knopf, 2024), 16-17.
3. Mary Oliver, "How I Go to the Woods" from *Swan: Poems and Prose Poems* (Beacon Press, 2010). Reprinted by the permission of The Charlotte Sheedy Literary Agency as agent for the Estate of the author. Copyright © 2010 by Mary Oliver with permission of Bill Reichblum.
4. C. S. Lewis, *Surprised by Joy: The Shape of My Early Life* (HarperOne, 2017).
5. One of the Buddha's sayings in the Dhammapada.
6. Jack Kornfield. *A Path with Heart: A Guide Through the Perils and Promises of Spiritual Life* (Bantam Books, 1993), 48-49. Revised for retelling in this book.
7. Author's version of a traditional story retold by Michael Meade.
8. Barry Lopez, *Crow and Weasel* (Square Fish, 1998).

To Serve and to Care

1. The original story can be found in Leo Tolstoy, *What Men Live by, and Other Tales*, trans. Aylmer Maude and Louise Shanks Maude (Legare Street Press, 2023).
2. Chris Whitmore, excerpt from "Readers Write In" from *The Sun* (February 2014). Reprinted with the permission of the author.

3. Terry Dobson, "The Aikido of Love." Reprinted with the permission of Riki Moss.
4. Lori Armstrong and Janet Lutz, "We Go Around and We Bless the Hands of All the People Who Work in the Hospital," Story Corps, originally aired on NPR's *Morning Edition*, December 19, 2008, storycorps.org/stories/janet-lutz-and-her-friend-lori-armstrong/.
5. One of the Buddha's sayings in the Dhammapada.
6. Alison Luterman, "At the Corner Store," *Sun Magazine*, December 2002, thesunmagazine.org/articles/24700-selected-poems.
7. Edmund D. Fountain and Trip Gabriel, "'Cajun Navy' Scours Houston Floodwaters for Stranded Residents," *New York Times*, August 30, 2017, archive.nytimes.com/www.nytimes.com/2017/08/30/us/cajun-navy-brings-its-rescue-fleet-to-houstons-flood-zone.html.
8. Story originally published in Christina Feldman and Jack Kornfield, ed., *Stories of the Spirit, Stories of the Heart: Parables of the Spiritual Path from Around the World* (HarperCollins, 1991). Revised for retelling in this book.
9. Molly Ivins, "The Fun's in the Fight," *Mother Jones*, May/June 1993, motherjones.com/politics/1993/05/funs-fight/.
10. Scott Z. Burns, *What's Possible: The U.N. Climate Summit Film*, directed by Louie Schwartzberg, produced by Lyn Lear, presented in New York at the United Nations Climate Summit on September 23, 2014, YouTube video, youtube.com/watch?v=MVyuh-vjZTE.

Mystery, Death, and Consciousness

1. "The Weight of a Snowflake," in *Peacemaking: Day By Day* (Pax Christi USA, 1985).
2. Juan Ramón Jiménez, "I Am Not I" from *Lorca and Jiménez: Selected Poems*, translated by Robert Bly. Copyright © 1973, 1997 by Robert Bly, © 1967 by Sixties Press. Reprinted with permission from Beacon Press, Boston, Massachusetts, and Georges Borchardt, Inc. on behalf of the translator's estate.
3. Story originally published in Jack Kornfield, *A Path with Heart: A Guide Through the Perils and Promises of Spiritual Life* (Bantam Books, 1993). Revised for retelling in this book.
4. Thich Nhat Hanh, "Contemplation of No-Coming and No-Going," in *No Death, No Fear: Comforting Wisdom for Life* (Riverhead Books, 2003).
5. Mary Oliver, "The Buddha's Last Instruction" from *House of Light* (Beacon Press, 1990). Reprinted by the permission of The Charlotte Sheedy Literary Agency as agent for the author. Copyright © 1990, 2010, 2017 by Mary Oliver with permission of Bill Reichblum.

Permissions

"Contemplation of No-Coming, No-Going" from *Chanting from the Heart: Buddhist Ceremonies and Daily Practices* by Thich Nhat Hanh and the monks and nuns of Plum Village. Copyright © 2007 by Unified Buddhist Church. Reprinted with the permission of The Permissions Company, LLC on behalf of Parallax Press, Berkeley, California, parallax.org.

Alison Luterman, "At the Corner Store." Reprinted with the permission of the author.

Allen Ginsberg, excerpt from "Footnote to Howl" from *Collected Poems 1944-1980*. Copyright © by Allen Ginsberg. Reprinted by permission of HarperCollins Publishers.

Chris Whitmore, excerpt from "Readers Write In" from *The Sun* (February 2014). Reprinted with the permission of the author.

Deena Metzger, excerpt from "Leavings" from *Ruin and Beauty: New and Selected Poems*. Copyright © 1989, 2009 by Deena

Metzger. Reprinted with the permission of The Permissions Company, LLC on behalf of Red Hen Press, redhen.org.

Jack Kornfield, adapted excerpt from *A Path with Heart: A Guide Through the Perils and Promises of Spiritual Life.* Copyright © 1993 by Jack Kornfield. Used by permission of Bantam Books, an imprint and division Penguin Random House, LLC. All rights reserved.

Juan Ramón Jiménez, "I Am Not I" from *Lorca and Jiménez: Selected Poems*, translated by Robert Bly. Copyright © 1973, 1997 by Robert Bly, © 1967 by Sixties Press. Reprinted with permission from Beacon Press, Boston, Massachusetts and Georges Borchardt, Inc. on behalf of the translator's estate.

Laszlo Slomovits, "Strangers" from *Rattle 60* (Summer, 2018). Reprinted with the permission of the author.

Mary Oliver, "How I Go to the Woods" from *Swan: Poems and Prose Poems* (Beacon Press, 2010). Reprinted by the permission of The Charlotte Sheedy Literary Agency as agent for the Estate of the author. Copyright © 2010 by Mary Oliver with permission of Bill Reichblum.

Mary Oliver, "The Buddha's Last Instruction" from *House of Light* (Beacon Press, 1990). Reprinted by the permission of The Charlotte Sheedy Literary Agency as agent for the author. Copyright © 1990, 2010, 2017 by Mary Oliver with permission of Bill Reichblum.

Mary Oliver, "What Can I Say" from *Swan: Poems and Prose Poems* (Beacon Press, 2010). Reprinted by the permission of The Charlotte Sheedy Literary Agency as agent for the Estate of the author. Copyright © 2010 by Mary Oliver with permission of Bill Reichblum.

Richard Selzer, excerpt from "The Surgeon as Priest" from *Mortal Lessons: Notes on the Art of Surgery*. Copyright © 1974, 1975, 1976, 1987 by Richard Selzer. Used by permission of Georges Borchardt, Inc. on behalf of the author's estate.

Rick Fields, "The Very Short Sutra on the Meeting of the Buddha and the Goddess" from *Dharma Gaia: A Harvest of Essays in Buddhism and Ecology*, edited by Allan Hunt-Badiner. Copyright © 1995 by Rick Fields. Reprinted with the permission of Marcia Fields.

Rumi, "Tell Me, What Have I Lost?" translated by Robert Bly, from *The Winged Energy of Delight: Selected Translations*. Copyright © 2004 by Robert Bly. Used by permission of HarperCollins Publishers and Georges Borchardt, Inc. on behalf of the translator's estate.

Terry Dobson, "The Aikido of Love." Reprinted with the permission of Riki Moss.

About the Author

JACK KORNFIELD trained as a Buddhist monk in the monasteries of Thailand, India, and Burma. He has taught meditation internationally since 1974 and is one of the key teachers to introduce Buddhist mindfulness practice to the West. Jack cofounded the Insight Meditation Society in Barre, Massachusetts, and the Spirit Rock Center in Woodacre, California. He holds a PhD in clinical psychology and is a husband, grandfather, and activist. His seventeen books have sold two million copies and have been translated into twenty-two languages. They include *The Wise Heart: A Guide to the Universal Teachings of Buddhist Psychology*; *A Path with Heart*; *After the Ecstasy, the Laundry*; *The Art of Forgiveness, Lovingkindness, and Peace*; and *No Time Like the Present*. For more, visit jackkornfield.com.

To hear a whole course of stories on which this book is based, use this QR code:

About Sounds True

SOUNDS TRUE was founded in 1985 by Tami Simon with a clear mission: to disseminate spiritual wisdom. Since starting out as a project with one woman and her tape recorder, we have grown into a multimedia publishing company with a catalog of more than 3,000 titles by some of the leading teachers and visionaries of our time, and an ever-expanding family of beloved customers from across the world.

In more than four decades of evolution, Sounds True has maintained our focus on our overriding purpose and mission: to wake up the world. We offer books, audio programs, online learning experiences, and in-person events to support your personal growth and awakening, and to unlock our greatest human capacities to love and serve.

At SoundsTrue.com you'll find a wealth of resources to enrich your journey, including our weekly *Insights at the Edge* podcast, free downloads, and information about our nonprofit Sounds True Foundation, where we strive to remove financial barriers to the materials we publish through scholarships and donations worldwide.

To learn more, please visit SoundsTrue.com/freegifts or call us toll-free at 800.333.9185.

Together, we can wake up the world.